The Final Broken Piece

A Novel by:

Beverly N. Vercher

Copyright © by Beverly N. Vercher
All rights reserved. No part of this book may be used or reproduced, stored, or transmitted in any manner whatsoever without written permission from Beverly N. Vercher.

DEDICATION

To God,
Thank you for blessing me with this gift to write and this gift a creativity.
Without you, I am nothing.

To my children, John, Johnae, Jahquela, and my grandchildren, Niyah, and Anna...this is for you. I strive for greatness everyday for you. My love for you can not be described in any words in any book. You are my world.

To my husband, Anthony (Troy), thank you for being my backbone. I appreciate you and I love you dearly.

To Tequila Joseph & Stephanie Cohens, Thank you ladies for believing me and giving me the push I needed to start this project.
I love you both!

The Final Broken Piece   Beverly N. Vercher

INTRODUCTION

Just when we thought the story has ended. So many twists and turns brought us right back to the brokenness. In this third edition to the sequel (Good Hearts are the Easiest Broken pt 1, Shattered but not Broken pt 2), Priscilla is faced head on with dealing with her past molestation by her deceased mother's boyfriend through one of her clients. As one of the most influential African American Psychiatrists in America, she takes on a client that will remind her of the brokenness that lead to her mother's death and she will have to deal with it in a way she never imagined.

Over the years, everyone had seemed to find their happiness but a few things happened that will shock you.

It will put her and her brother Shawn, who decided to drop Jr from his name, in a position that will have you wondering if their relationship would be threatened. You'll find out if their family is really as strong as it seems or if they will fall apart.

I hope you enjoy part three as much as you did the first two parts of this sequel. Thank you so much for your support. It is greatly appreciated!

Happy Reading!!

Beverly N. Vercher

Chapter One

Priscilla watched Camille play with her doll. It was her third session with the seven year old and she hasn't had a conversation with her yet. The little girl was brought to her by her mother who stated that she stopped talking all of a sudden. One day she was the bubbly playful little girl and the next, she wouldn't say one word and it's been that way for quite some time.

"It has been over six months since the last time I heard my daughter's voice other than when she cries. I don't know what to do." Her mother, Jasmine, said as she wiped the tears from her face.

"Prior this, did she have any episodes of acting out or crying for no reason?" Priscilla asked.

"The only thing that changed she has become extremely clingy to me. Before this, she would sit and play alone. We would have our mommy-daughter time. I would paint her nails and we'd have a

tea party. For the most part, she played by herself. But now she wants to be near me at all times. She even started wanting me to sleep in her bed with her. I just don't understand what's going on." Jasmine said.

"How is she with her father or other members of the family?" Priscilla asked.

"She's gotten to the point where she doesn't want to be around anyone. Not even her father and they used to have a great relationship. She was truly a daddy's girl but all that has changed too. Please help me Dr. Walton." Jasmine said.

Priscilla promised Jasmine that she would do everything she could to help Camille.

     *   *   *

By their sixth visit, Priscilla was able to get her to interact by coloring. It was their first session without her mother there. All the previous sessions included her because Camille would cry and scream when Jasmine would try to leave the room.

On this day, Priscilla didn't even budge when her mother got up to leave. She immediately came in and headed for the table where the coloring book and crayons were already laying out.

For a while Priscilla simply watched, then she joined the little girl at the table and asked if she could color with her. She nodded.

Because of her past as well as her education, Priscilla already had a feeling about what was going on with her. She felt that her father or someone else was molesting her. She didn't want to say anything to Jasmine until she was able to get the little girl to open up. This was going to be the start of a long road and the steps had to be taken carefully.

As Priscilla colored in one of the books, she continued to watch Camille. She noticed that she would only color the pages with the mother and child. She always skipped the ones that included the father.

"*Camille, let's color this page together.*" Priscilla asked.

It was a photo of the mom, dad, and child together. Camille shook her head and slid her chair away from the table.

"*It's okay. We don't have to color that page. Look...I got rid of it altogether.*" Priscilla said and ripped the page from the book.

Camille came back to the table and they continued to color together.

Chapter Two

"*Look, we have an agreement and I expect you to stick to it!*" Shawn yelled in the phone.

"*I don't think I'm being unreasonable Shawn. I just need a little more help with our daughter. I agreed that you would stay invisible and allow my husband to raise her as his own. I'm just asking for a little more help and you should be glad to do it.*" The woman on the other end replied.

"*Okay okay but this is it! I'm not doing nothing else! Don't call me no damn more!*" He said then hung up the phone.

One damn mistake and I have to put up with this shit! He said out loud, then threw his phone on the desk.

"*What shit?*" Lori said as she entered his office.

Lori and Shawn had been married fifteen years. They met through mutual friends at a wedding and two years later, they were married.

"Just work stuff baby." He said as he walked to her. He gave her a hug then kissed her on the forehead.

"Even though you work from home, sometimes I still feel like you're far away. Let's go out for lunch." She said.

"Well baby, I'm home but I still have just as much work to do; but right now, lunch sounds good." He replied.

*   *   *   *

Lori knew exactly who her husband was talking to and she knew about this love child he had. She was waiting for the perfect moment to confront him but she had to think of the right words to say.

Although she was hurt, she still loved her husband, and she remembered the one thing her mom told her the night before she got married: *"No man is perfect. Only God is so don't expect him to always do the right thing. He will make mistakes and it will devastate you. I'm not saying to stick by him making the same mistake over and over again but there will be times that you have to forgive him and move on."*

Lori knew that she would eventually say something but not right then. She just wanted to enjoy his company. Because of their work schedules, they didn't get to spend a lot of time together so when they were able to, she wanted it to be enjoyable.

    *   *   *   *

"You know I love you, right?" Shawn said.

"Yes and I love you too." Lori replied.

"I mean really. You're the best thing that's ever happened to me. I can't imagine my life without you in it." He said.

For a moment, Lori thought that he was working his way up to telling her about the mystery child that he had. She thought for sure that a big *"But"* was coming at the end of the statement. She prayed that he would some day tell her.

"I love you too. You are the love of my life and I can't imagine my

life without you either." She said and she meant it wholeheartedly. *"Lori, there's something I need to tell you and I know that it's going to hurt you. But I want you to know that I've never done and never will do anything to purposely hurt you. I'm just a man that made a big mistake and I feel that it's time to tell you so that we can work it out and move past it."* Shawn said as he looked his wife in her eyes.

She just nodded.

"A few years ago, when I was away on that seven month assignment I had an affair. It was during the first two months, time period that I wasn't able to come home and you weren't able to come visit. I was lonely and I met this young lady at a bar one night and after communicating with her for a while, she and I got involved in a sexual relationship. It only lasted a little while and we never had any intentions of making it anything more than sex because she's married too. Well, she found out she was pregnant,

we had a paternity test, and the child is mine. She and I made an agreement that she would let her husband raise the child as his own and I would pay her child support every month. I'm so sorry that it's taken me so long to tell you this. I wanted to so badly but the timing was never right. I know you have lots of questions and I promise that I'll answer every one of them." He said.

"I appreciate you for finally coming to me and telling me about this. I've been over the pain for quite some time and now I can move forward with forgiving you." She said.

He looked surprised as she continued to explain to him that she had known about the child for nearly two years.

Chapter Three

Priscilla sat in her office with the lights off. She made it a habit of taking some time to meditate during the day to free herself of all the sad and negative energies she has to encounter. She does this for twenty minutes every day on her lunch break then again at the end of the before going home.

It has always worked for her but she has not been able to get Camille off her mind. The connection she had with that little girl is so strong that she finds herself thinking about her all the time.

I have to help her, she said out loud.

Priscilla remembered how drawing in her books exposed the painful secret of her abuse, so she decided to go that same direction with Camille.

When her alarm sounded, signalizing that she have five minutes before her next appointment, she opened the blinds to allow the light back in.

"Dr. Walton, your one o'clock his here." Her assistant, Amanda said through the phone.

"You can bring them in." Priscilla replied.

"Well, hello beautiful." Priscilla said when Camille came through the door. She simply waved.

"I'm just going to be out here, okay." Her mom said before closing the door.

Camille walked over to the table where she always colors but instead of a coloring book and a pile of crayons, there was a book and one red crayon. She stood there with a confused look on her face.

The book was "Some Secrets Should Never Be Kept By Jayneen Sanders", a children's book about a little boy being molested.

"Camille, you and I have had a lot of fun during our sessions but it's time that I talk to you. I think I know why you stopped talking

and I want you to know that it happened to me too when I was a little girl. I know that you are scared but you don't have to be. Your mother and I will protect you but, baby, we need you to talk." She said.

Tears rolled down Camille's face as she shook her head no.

"Okay look, I got you this book to read and I want you to do something else. Every time it happens, I want you to put a mark in the back of this book. It can be any kind of mark you want. When it happened to me, I drew sad faces. Can you draw a sad face?" She asked holding the book in her hand.

She handed the little girl the crayon and although she resisted at first, Priscilla got her to draw a sad face on the last page of the book.

"Now, I want you to do this every time it happens and I want you to bring this book with you the next time you come to see me?

The Final Broken Piece   Beverly N. Vercher

Keep it in your backpack so that you won't forget it, okay?" Priscilla said fighting back the tears. She hated sending her back with her mother knowing that she could potentially be molested by her father every day for the next week but she needed proof before she could take her next steps; which involved getting child protective services involved.

        *   *   *

"Hey honey. You've seemed a little distracted the past few weeks. Are you okay?" Kevin asked.

Priscilla and Kevin were high school sweethearts who got married two years after graduating college. They were best friends and knew each other better than anyone else in the world. So she wasn't surprised at what he said.

"Yes, I'm okay. I just can't get one of my patients off my mind." She replied.

"Really, why?" **He asked.**

"She reminds me of me and what I went through as a child.." She said.

Kevin knew exactly what she meant by that. Priscilla had given him all the heartbreaking details of her past. Her father's incarceration, her molestation, and her mother's suicide. He felt that she was the strongest person he had ever known. When they met in high school, he never would have know that this kind and compassionate person had been through so much.

"Wow, baby. What are you going to do?" He asked then kissed her hand.

"I have a game plan but I have to make sure that I do things exactly right. Not only to protect her but I want to make sure that her mother is protected as well." She said.

"I know that you will make the right decision. God sent her to you for a reason and you just have to trust that he will help you along the way." He said.

"Thanks honey. You're right. I just have to pray about it." She said.

Before going to bed, Priscilla prayed for Camille and her mother. She reflected on her abuse and how it affected her mother. Losing her mother was the hardest thing she ever had to live with. She felt that it was harder to heal from the the actual abuse.

Chapter Four

"You've been taking her to this damn therapist for almost four months now and she still ain't talking. Why don't you just leave it alone? She'll talk when she gets ready. Ain't that right princess." Manny said.

He reached out to touch his daughter but she jerked away from him and squeezed her mother tight.

"Dr. Walton seems to be getting through to her now. Camille is no longer resistant when I try to leave the room and see actually smiles when I mention that she has an appointment. Although she hasn't actually spoken to her yet, they seem to communicate. Camille is starting to trust her and I feel that if we're patient she'll start talking again. Then maybe we'll learn why she stopped in the first place." Jasmine said.

"I think it's a waste of time but whatever." He said then left the room.

*   *   *

Later that night, Camille was sleeping soundly in her room. She didn't realize that he mother had left the and was already in a deep sleep in her own bed.

Manny slid beside her and she cuddled closer to him thinking that it was her mother. He laid with her for a while; smelling her hair and enjoying the feeling of her small body next to his.

The guilt of what he'd done would eat him up inside afterward but he just couldn't stop the urges so when they came, nothing could stop him.

Camille jumped when she felt him pulling her panties down.

"Shhh princess. It's just me, daddy." He said.

Camille knew the drill. She laid down, flat on her back and let her father touch her. Tears ran from her eyes as the pain of his fingers entering her, ran through her body. It was the longest ten minutes of her life. She had to lay there and let him touch her as he rubbed himself until he was done.

"You know you can't tell that doctor about our secret, right? And if you decide to never talk again, it's okay too but you have to stop being mean to daddy around your mother or she's going to figure out what's going on and then she'll hate you. She will get mad at you and send you away. Do you want that?" He asked.

She shook her head.

"No go back to sleep and I'll see you in the morning." He said.

She waited until she heard his footsteps disappear up the hall and the door to the room he shared with her mom close. Then she placed the pillow over her head and screamed to the top of her lungs.

*   *   *

"Good morning baby. Are you ready to eat breakfast?" Jasmine asked.

Camille never looked up at her mother. She just went to the kitchen table and waited for her meal. The sound of her father walking up the hall made her skin crawl. He walked over to the table, kissed her on the head and said, *"Good morning princess."* It took everything in her to resist the urge to run to her mother but she remembered what he had said so she sat still.

Once breakfast was over, she went to her room, found her book bag, and pulled the book out that Dr. Walton had given her. She read a few pages then she turned it to the very last page and drew a sad face.

*   *   *

"Dr. Walton, your two o'clock appointment is here." Amanda said through the phone.

"Great, bring them in." Priscilla said.

Jasmine and Camille entered the room and, as always, Jasmine waited a few seconds to make sure her daughter would be alright with her leaving the room and once she was sure it was fine, she left back out and closed the door.

"Hi Camille, how are you?" Priscilla asked.

Camille started down at her lap. Priscilla wanted to ask about the book so badly but she didn't want to risk the chance of moving too fast.

"Are you in the mood to talk or do you want to color? I have some new coloring books for you." Priscilla said.

Camille went to the table where the new books and crayons were laying and sat down. Priscilla noticed how more protective of her book bag she was that day. She normally puts it down but on this day, she's keeping it very close to her.

"So did you get a chance to read the book I gave you? If not, I can read a few pages to you or maybe you can read some to me. How about that?" Priscilla said.

Camille slowly reached for her bag. Her heart was racing as she unzipped it and pulled the book out. Her little hands trembled as she reached it across the table.

Priscilla's hands were shaking just as badly as she held the book. Before opening it, she closed her eyes and asked God for the strength to see what's inside.

Tears streamed down her face when she flipped the last page as saw eight little sad faces drawn by the little girl sitting in front of her.

"Are you ready to talk to me?" Priscilla asked.

After nearly a year of not speaking, she said, *"Yes."*

Chapter Five

"So you've know all this time and haven't come to me. Why and how did you find out?" Shawn asked.

"It was truly a coincidence. I was in your office cleaning when I heard a phone vibrating in your file cabinet. I just knew that you had gotten so busy that you ran out and forgot it. That was until I opened the drawer and saw this it was a totally different phone. So I picked it up and saw that you had some text messages. Now, normally I would have assumed that you had found someone's phone and just placed I back. But something compelled me to read the messages. I was able to get all the information I wanted because you never deleted any of the messages between the two of you. But the messages that day were about her trying to convince you to change your mind about the terms of your agreement. She wanted you to consider being in the child's life. I wanted to say something to you but at the same time, I felt that

you should tell me. This wasn't something I should have found out any other way so I decided to ignore it until you were ready to talk to me about it. But I have a question. Did you ever go meet with her?" Lori said.

Shawn Sr shook his head and said, *"No I didn't. Baby, I still can't understand how you've known this for two years and didn't ask me about it."*

"There were many times that I wanted to but I prayed about it and I was waiting on God to give me the word." She said.

He knew that she was telling the truth. His wife was the most faithful and spiritual woman, besides his grandmother, that he'd ever met.

"The only thing I'm having an issue with is the fact that you have a child in this world that doesn't know you even exist. That doesn't sit right with me. She should have her father. Her real

father in her life and now that I know, we can make that happen." She continued.

"Baby, I'm not sure about that. I mean, I'm glad you know and it's all out in the open. You just don't understand how this has been eating me up inside but I don't want to bring any unnecessary drama in our lives. What if you and her mother doesn't get along? What if she starts being demanding? I won't let this come between what you and I have built. If that means letting her husband raise the child as his own, that's what it will be. I'll just continue sending her the monthly support as agreed." He said.

*　　*　　*

"Priscilla, he would kill me if he knows that I told you but I had to talk to someone about it." Lori said.

She and her sister in law, Priscilla, have lunch every Saturday to catch up. And they definitely had a lot to catch up on.

"I just can't believe this. I'm in shock. My little brother has a child. Really?" Priscilla replied.

"Just imagine how I felt when I found out. But, I have forgiven him. I love my husband. I know that he's not perfect but I know that he'll never do anything to purposely hurt me. My problem is with this agreement. How are we suppose to just let this child grow up never knowing her father? I mean, it may be his only chance at being a father." Lori said fighting back tears.

Priscilla hugged her and said, *"I'm so sorry Lori. I know this is hard for you. Your prayers are powerful and I'm proof that they activate blessings. God will give you a child of your own. You must believe that."* Priscilla said.

"I do believe that but I also believe that a child of my own may not come from my womb." Lori replied.

"I just don't understand why he's kept this secret from us. I mean, I do understand that he didn't want to hurt you but why not come to me?" Priscilla asked.

"I don't know. Maybe he thought you would be disappointed." Lori said.

"Disappointed? No! I'm just shocked. I have so many questions right now." Priscilla said.

"Please promise me that you won't say anything. He will be so mad if he knew that I told you. It took awhile but he finally told me so maybe you're next." Lori said.

"Maybe." Priscilla said.

"Well enough about that. How are the kids?" Lori asked.

"They're doing great. Shay and Shemar are playing softball now and Dominic is still my little reader." Priscilla replied.

"Awe, they are growing up so fast. It's like I don't see them for a couple of weeks and they grow three inches and have all new interests." Lori laughed.

"I know right. The twins are always trying something new but Dominic is still a bookworm." Priscilla said.

"And how's Kevin?" Lori asked.

"He's good too. Working like crazy but the good thing is that it's finally starting to pay off. His law firm is growing and he's even secured his first big client so hopefully he'll be able to slow down." Priscilla said.

"That's wonderful and you. How are you doing?" Lori asked.

"I'm good." Priscilla replied.

"Just good? Everyone else was great. What's going on?" Lori asked.

"I can't go into detail but I have a new client that is making me relive my abuse and my mother's death. I look at her and she reminds me so much of me that it's eerie. I think she's getting abused by her father and if that is true. Her life is about to get turned upside down." Priscilla said.

"Oh my goodness, Priscilla. I will definitely keep you and her in my prayers. Lean on God for your strength my sister. You know that he'll never lead you to a place and leave you. This is part of your purpose. You do know that right?" Lori said.

"Yes, I know. I've been praying constantly. Not for me but for her and her mother. I just want to make sure that I make the right decisions when I confirm that it's true. My next appointment with her is this week. So expect to find out then." Priscilla replied.

"You and God will make the right decision." Lori said.

The women changed the subject and spent the rest of the afternoon making plans to see each other again and possibly going on a family vacation together.

Chapter Six

"Come in Officer Roberts and thank you for meeting with me today." Priscilla said.

"Of course. I knew that it was important so I rushed right over." Officer Roberts replied.

Being that the situation was so delicate, Priscilla thought having a female officer take on the case would be better. She hoped that Camille would feel more comfortable with her.

"Yes it is important. This is a very serious situation. I have a seven year old client who, I strongly believe, is being molested by her father." Priscilla said fighting back tears. In her profession, she knew better than to get emotionally involved in her cases but she felt a connection with Camille the first day she walked in her office.

"The first thing we need to do is get her out of the home. I need to call my contact, Mrs. Ferguson, at CPS. Do you mind?" Officer Roberts asked as she reached for her cellphone.

"No, please do. Hopefully she can come or send someone now." Priscilla said.

"I'll ask." Officer Roberts said.

While the officer was on the phone, Priscilla sat at her desk thinking about Camille and Jasmine. Then thoughts of her own mother crossed her mind. She closed her eyes and began to silently pray:

Dear God, I come to you today asking for strength...physically, mentally, and emotionally as I attempt to help this little girl and her mother. I'm asking that you guide my steps so that I do what's right for this family. Please keep them both covered under the blood of Jesus so that when this is all over, they can be whole and not broken. We need you Lord. Amen

After praying, she felt better. Her grandmother, Pastor Rachel, taught her and Shawn about the importance of prayer at a very young age.

Priscilla knew that everyone would do all they could to protect Camille and to make sure she gets the help she needs. But she wanted to make sure Jasmine doesn't get lost in the process.

*   *   *

"Mrs. Ferguson is on her way right now. She should be here in less than thirty minutes." Office Roberts said.

"Great." Priscilla replied.

"You look a little uneasy. I know this is a tough situation to deal with but unfortunately, it's pretty common in my profession. We do our best to work hand in hand with CPS to make sure that the

child gets the protection and help they need." Officer Roberts said.

"I know that the most important thing is to make sure that Camille is okay but what about her mother? She's a victim too and will need help dealing with the trauma of what happened to her little girl." Priscilla said.

Officer Roberts could see the passion in Priscilla's eyes. *"I know that cases like this are hard and it's easy to get emotionally involved but, Dr. Walton, you can't let this get to you. Once CPS takes over, your job is done and you will have nothing else to do with Camille, her mother, or this case. Do you understand that?"*

Priscilla sat quietly for a moment. She fought back the tears welling up in her eyes. She took a few deep breaths and before she knew it, she was telling Officer Roberts about her abuse as a child and her mother's death. By the time she was finished, the tears she was fighting so hard to hold back, were running down her face.

"That's why I'm so emotionally attached to this child and so adamant about getting her mother help." Priscilla explained.

Before Officer Robert could reply, Priscilla's phone rang. It was her assistant advising that Mrs. Ferguson with CPS had arrived.

Chapter Seven

"I will have the child removed from the home immediately and I assume you will pick the father up." Mrs. Ferguson said to Priscilla and Officer Roberts.

"I will talk to the judge when I leave here but as you know, there are steps we need to take before we can get a warrant but as soon as it's signed, I'll pick him up." Officer Roberts replied.

"I've already expressed this to Officer Roberts but I want to make sure that her mother, Jasmine, gets the help she'll need during this time as well. Does CPS offer assistance for the parents?" Priscilla said.

*"Yes we do. There's a program that provides counseling for parents with children in foster care. As long as she's not implicated in the abuse, they will make sure she has regular visits with her child and they will have some counseling sessions

together as well. Look Dr. Walton, I understand your concern but our first priority is the child's safety. Now, once her mother is cleared, we will help her and get her child back home." Mrs. Ferguson explained.

Priscilla didn't say anything but she thought to herself, *"When did you start doing that?"* She was frustrated but she knew that her hands were tied.

Before the ladies left, Officer Roberts promised to give her a call with an update.

*   *   *   *

"Hey mom. How are you?" Priscilla said. She had come up with an idea and hoped that her mother, Sheryl would agree.

"I'm good, how are you?" Sheryl replied.

"I really need to talk to you. Do you mind if I come by?" Priscilla asked.

"Honey you know that you don't have to ask to come by. Besides, Tia would be excited to see you." Sheryl said.

"I know that I don't need permission but I know that you and Malcolm stay on the go." Priscilla laughed the continued, *"And tell Tia that I miss her."*

"You're right but we don't have any plans this evening." Sheryl laughed as well.

Priscilla heard Sheryl call for Tia. *"Tia! Tia! Tiana! Come her, your sister is on the phone!"*

"Yay!" Tia yelled then Priscilla could hear her running down the stairs.

"Hello! Hey sissy! I miss you. When are you coming over?" Tia asked.

"Hello sweetie. I'm actually coming over shortly. I miss you." Priscilla said.

"Yay! I miss you too. I can't wait to see you. Here's mom." Tia said then gave the phone back to Sheryl.

"That girl loves her sister, honey." She said.

"I love her too. I can't believe that she's already in High School. She's growing up so fast." Priscilla said.

"I know right. She's growing up just as fast as you and Shawn. did. Well, I'll see you shortly." Sheryl said.

Priscilla called Kevin, her husband, to let him know that she was going to be late.

"Okay honey. Be careful and I'll see you when you get home." He said.

Before she had even put the car in park, Priscilla saw Tia standing at the door waving. She noticed how much her little sister was growing up to look so much like Sheryl. She had Malcolm's eyes but everything else was all Sheryl.

"Hey sissy!" Tia said as she hugged Priscilla.

"Hello my pretty little sister." Priscilla replied.

"Mom is in the kitchen." Tia said then grabbed Priscilla's free hand and led her to the kitchen here Sheryl was making tea.

"Hello mom." Priscilla said as she kissed Sheryl on the cheek and handed her a bouquet of flowers that she had stopped and purchased on the way. She always brought flowers whenever she went to see her mother and her grandmother.

"Hey beautiful." Sheryl replied as he hugged Priscilla.

By the time Sheryl had gotten a good look at the flowers, Tia had already grabbed a crystal vase out of the cabinet.

Priscilla, Sheryl, and Tia sat at the table chatting for a few minutes. Priscilla really enjoyed spending time with her little sister but she really needed to talk to her mother.

"Hey Sis, I'm going to come pick you up Saturday and we're going to get pedicures. How about that?" Priscilla said.

"Oh my God, YES!" Tia said, barely able to contain her excitement.

Priscilla smiled and said, "Great. I have something very important to speak with mom about to can you please give us a little privacy? I promise to see you before I leave."

"Okay." Tia said sadly.

They ladies sat quietly until they heard Tia's door closed but before Priscilla began to speak, Malcolm came down stairs.

"Sorry to interrupt ladies. I'm just grabbing a drink.." He said then hugged Priscilla and kissed Sheryl.

"Hello Malcolm. How are you?" She replied.

"Pretty good thanks. How is Kevin and the kids? We have to get together soon. It's been too long." He said.

"They're great. As you can imagine, the kids are getting big but you're right. Maybe mom, grandmother, and I can plan a big Sunday dinner soon?" Priscilla said then looked at Sheryl.

"Sounds good to me." Malcolm replied then headed back but the stairs just as quickly as he had come down.

Chapter Eight

Jasmine, Camille, and Manny were sitting at the table having breakfast when there was a knock at the door.

"Hi, I'm Elaine Ferguson, this is my assistant, Marissa Dunn and were from Child Protective Services, and this is Officer Roberts from the police department. Are you Mr. Rollins?" Mrs. Ferguson said.

"Yes, I'm Mr. Rollins. What is this about?" Manny replied.

"May we come in and speak with you and Mrs. Rollins?" Mrs. Ferguson asked.

Manny opened the door wider and motioned for them to come in. *"You can have a seat here and I'll go get my wife."* He replied.

As he walked into the kitchen Jasmine asked, *"Who was at the door?"*

"Child protective services and the police." He said as he stared at Camille. She never looked up from her plate.

"What? Who?" Jasmine said.

"They want to talk to us." Manny said.

Jasmine had Camille go to her room while she and Manny went in the living room.

"I know that you're wondering why we made this surprise visit and I'll explain everything and answer any questions that both of you may have. Okay?" Mrs. Ferguson explained.

Jasmine and Manny nodded.

"We were contacted by Dr. Walton because she suspects that your daughter, Camille has been abused. Apparently, you took her to counseling, Mrs. Rollins, because she had stopped talking and after a few sessions, Dr. Walton states that your daughter expressed this to her and that her father, Mr. Rollins was the person doing it to her." Mrs. Ferguson said.

"How the hell are you going to sit in my home and accuse me of abusing my own daughter? I told you not to take her to that damn doctor in the first place! Just because she doesn't want to talk doesn't mean anything is wrong with her! Now you got some damn doctor that I haven't even met saying this shit about me! Get out! I need all of you too leave now!" Manny was so angry that his voice was raised and he was standing up.

Officer Roberts stood up as well and placed her hand on her taser. *"Calm down Mr. Rollins."*

"What do you mean, calm down. You come here accusing me of hurting my little girl and I'm supposed to calm down? Hell no! I need you and these other two people to leave now!" He yelled.

"Mr. Rollins we can't do that until we're finished speaking with you, Mrs. Rollins, and Camille. I assure you the police department and the Child Protective Service will work together and make sure this case is thoroughly investigated." Office Roberts said.

"Our jobs is to insure the safety and security of Camille. Now if it's found that these claims are false, we will do all that we can to get your lives back to normal." Mrs. Ferguson explained.

Jasmine sat quietly with tears streaming down her face. Although she had a thousand thoughts going through her head, she was speechless.

Manny sat back down beside her and placed his hand on hers. She slowly moved it away. Mrs. Ferguson made a note of this subtle gesture.

"I also want to let you know that until the investigation is complete, Camille will be removed from the home. She will be placed in foster care and she undergo a physical and psychological evaluations." Mrs. Ferguson said.

By the time she finished speaking, Jasmine was crying very loud and Manny was visibly upset but he sat quietly staring Mrs. Ferguson in her eyes.

She didn't feel threatened by him. This wasn't her first case like this and she knew that, sadly, it wouldn't be her last. Besides, Office Roberts was there to handle things if they get out of control. There also was another officer parked outside just in case they needed back up.

While getting the case together, they ran Manny's background check and found that he is a registered sex offender and had been imprisoned for molesting an old girlfriend's daughter. Although that doesn't mean that he molested his own daughter but they had to take in consideration that he is capable of committing this type of crime and many offenders often repeat their actions.

*   *   *

Mrs. Ferguson took Jasmine in the kitchen to question her while Officer Roberts continued to question Manny in the living room, and Marissa went in Camille's bedroom to ask her some questions.

Marissa entered the room and found Camille on her bed with headphones on that were connected to a tablet.

"Hi Camille. My name is Marissa." She said with a warm smile.

Camille waved then he removed her headphones.

"What are you watching?" Marissa asked.

Camille didn't speak. She just turned her tablet so that Marissa could see that she was watching Barbie videos on YouTube.

"Ooh Barbie. I loved her when I was a little girl. As a matter of fact, I still love her." Marissa said with a laugh.

Camille giggled.

"Camille, I came in here to talk to you about some things. I don't want you to be afraid. You are not in any trouble and once we finish, you can go back to your Barbie videos, okay." Marissa said.

Camille stared.

"I know that you haven't spoken in quite sometime but I really need you to talk to me today. Can you do that for me?" Marissa said.

Camille nodded. Marissa could see the fear in her eyes.

The Final Broken Piece   Beverly N. Vercher

"Camille do you feel safe at home?" Marissa asked.

The little girl sat quietly as she struggled to speak. *"Sometimes."* She whispered.

"When do you feel safe at home? It is when mommy is here or when daddy is here?" Marissa asked.

Camille didn't say anything. She just shook her head.

"Hey, it's okay sweetie. You can talk to me. I just want to make sure that you're safe." Marissa said.

After a three minute silence, Camille took a deep breath and said, *"I feel safe with mommy."*

"What about daddy? Is he mean to you? Does he hurt you?" Marissa asked.

Camille buried her face in her hands and began to cry. Marissa embraced her and told her that *everything was going to be alright.*

"He will never hurt you again. I just need you to tell me what happened so we can make him stop."

"I don't want mommy to be mad at me. He said that if I told, she would hate me and make me leave." Camille cried.

"Your mother would never hate you. She loves you and I'm sure that if she knew that he was hurting you, she would make him leave. Tell me how he hurts you." Marissa said.

Although she's heard hundred of stories like this, her heart breaks each time she has to listen to a little girl explain how she's being abused. Camille spoke clearly; her vocabulary was beyond a seven year old and Marissa knew that it would be vital to the case. So many people have gotten off abuse charges because the child is confused or unable to clearly explain what happened to them and that hurt Marissa more than anything. But not only could Camille speak clearly, she was smart, and they had good evidence of the crime. During their conversation, Camille shared that she hid a pair of her panties in her room because she didn't want her mother to find them. Normally she would bury them in the bottom of the trash but the last time it happened, the trash had been taken out and she was afraid that her mother would see them.

"Can you show me where they are sweetie?" Marissa asked. Camille walked to her toy box, moved a few stuffed animals around and pointed. Marissa followed her and saw a little pair of panties laying there and her heart started racing when she noticed a blood stain.

"I have to go get Officer Roberts. Please do not touch them. Leave them right there, okay." Marissa said and hurried out of the room. A few moments later they returned and found Camille sitting on her bed, with her knees to her chest, crying.

"Camille, it's going to be okay. I promise. You've done a great job sweetie and like I said, you will not get in trouble." Marissa said while hugging her.

Office Roberts put on a pair of gloves, grabbed the panties, and put them in an envelope. Then she went back to the living room where Manny was still waiting.

"Mr. Rollins, I need to take you to the station for questioning. Wait here for a moment." Officer Roberts stepped outside and called for backup.

Chapter Nine

Lori sat on the porch drinking coffee, as she did every morning. It was her way of meditating and getting ready for the day. For the past few weeks, all she could think about was her husband's daughter. She wanted to badly to meet the little girl but Shawn was totally against it. He wouldn't even tell her the child's name. She understood the agreement that he made with the mother but she doesn't agree with it. *A child should know her family.* She thought to herself.

"Good morning beautiful." Shawn said as he sat in the chair beside Lori. He always gave her about twenty minutes of alone time then he'd join her on the porch.

"Good morning." She replied and reached for his hand. He grabbed her petite hand and kissed it.

They sat quietly for a moment. Simply enjoying the beautiful view of their well kept backyard and the nice weather.

"What do you have planned for today?" Lori said.

"I'll probably be working for most of the day. I have some deadlines coming up and you know how that is. What do you have planned?" He replied.

"Priscilla and I are taking Mother Sheryl and Tia out to lunch. I was hoping you could come as well. We're planning a family vacation." She said.

"I'm good with whatever you all decide. Give them all my love. We're still having dinner with them next week, right?" He asked.

"Yes, She wants to cook but I told her that we're taking them out. Well, I have your schedule for the next few months so that will help with deciding on the dates for the vacation." Lori said.

"Okay dear. I have to get to work. See you later." Shawn said then kissed her forehead before going back into the house.

Lori stayed a little longer. Thoughts of the little girl kept coming to the forefront of her mind. She tried to let it go but not matter how hard she tried, she couldn't. She also wanted so badly to talk to Shawn about it and hopefully change his mind but he just wasn't having it. Feeling defeated, she decided to let it go for the moment.

*   *   *

"I'm so excited!" Tia said after the details of the family vacation were decided.

They were going to Cocoa Beach, Florida for six day and five nights the following month.

"We're going to have a great time and I'm looking forward to it as well." Sheryl said.

"I definitely need this vacation. The past few months have been stressful at work." Priscilla said.

"Oh honey I know." Lori said. She wanted to know if there was an update but she didn't ask because she felt the subject might have been too sensitive for Tia.

"Tia, Shawn and I are taking Mom, Malcolm, and Tia out for dinner on Sunday. You and Kevin should come and bring the kids. We having all gotten together in a very long time." Lori said.

"That sounds great." Sheryl said.

"We'll definitely be there." Priscilla said.

Sheryl could tell that something was bothering Priscilla. She had that same sad look in her eyes that she use to have when she was a little girl. *"Priscilla, are you okay? You have that look in your eyes."*

"Yes I'm okay. I'm just ready for this vacation. Kevin and I have been working a lot. Plus the kids. We all need a break." She replied with a forced laugh.

Lori laughed, she and Sheryl both knew Priscilla well enough to know that something else was wrong but they didn't say anything.

A few seconds later, Priscilla's phone rung. When she saw that it was from her assistant, Amanda, she excused herself.

"Hi Amanda, what's up?" She said.

"Hey Dr. Walton. I'm sorry to interrupt your lunch with your family but I have something very important to tell you and I need you to come back to the office and you might want to bring them with you." Amanda said.

"What's going on Amanda?" Priscilla asked.

"I can't tell you this over the phone. I really need you to come to the office or I can come to you." Amanda said.

"No, I'm on my way right now." Priscilla said.

"Okay and just to give you a head's up, Officer Roberts will be here too." Amanda said.

Priscilla stood there for a moment trying to figure out what was going on. Since Amanda mentioned Officer Roberts, she knew that it had to have something to do with Camille. She just didn't understand why she asked her to bring her family.

She rushed back to the table. Lori and Sheryl could see that she was shaken.

"What's wrong? What happened?" Sheryl asked.

"I, I don't know." Priscilla stuttered.

"Who was that on the phone?" Lori asked.

"It was my assistant Amanda." Priscilla said.

"What did she say? What's wrong Priscilla?" Sheryl asked in a panicked voice.

"We have to go to my office now. I don't know what's going on but she said that I need to come now and bring you all with me." Priscilla said.

"Come on let's go. Lori, do you mind driving? There's no way I'm letting Priscilla drive like this." Sheryl said. She wrapped her arm around Priscilla and asked Tia to take the other side.

By the time they had made it to the car, Priscilla had called Kevin, Sheryl called Pastor Rachel, and Lori called Shawn. They didn't know what was going on but they felt that the whole family should be there.

For the fifteen minute drive to her office, Tia held Priscilla. She laid her head on her big sister's chest and listened to the rapid beating of her heart. She knew that something very serious was happening. Her mom told her about her Aunt Tia, whom she was named after. She also told her how she died and why she killed herself but since she was born, she doesn't recall anything bad happening in their family so this situation had her afraid.

Priscilla took her seat belt off before the car came to a complete stop and by the time Lori had put the gear in park, she had already gotten out of the car.

Chapter Ten

Manny declined to make a statement to Officer Roberts. He asked to call his lawyer and Attorney Morrison arrived to the station thirty minutes after they did.

Jasmine was brought in for questioning as well.

"Hi Mrs. Rollins. I'm Officer Steadman and I just want to ask you a few questions, okay?"

Jasmine wiped the tears from her eyes. Her face was bright red and her eyes were swollen because of all the crying she had done.

"I just want to talk to you about your husband. How long have you been married?" He asked.

"Nine years." She said.

"And your daughter is seven, right?" He asked.

The tears fell harder from her eyes. *"Yes."* She replied.

"I'm just going to be honest with you Mrs. Rollins or can I call you Jasmine?" He asked.

"Jasmine is fine." She replied.

"We plan to arrest your husband for molesting your daughter and he'll be going to jail for a long time. Now, I don't want to upset you any more than you already are but these are questions that I have to ask. Did you know that your husband was sexually molesting your daughter?" He asked.

"No no no. Oh my God no! I can't believe he did that. My poor baby. Where is she? I know that she's scared. She needs me." Jasmine broke down crying uncontrollably. It took Officer Steadman quite some time to calm her down.

"She's going to be fine Jasmine and as soon as we get all this cleared up on your end, we can get you to her. Are you okay to continue?" He asked.

"Yes, I just want to get this over with so that I can get to her." She replied.

"You never saw any signs of the abuse. She didn't act differently around him?" He asked.

"No. Yes. Well now it all makes sense." She said.

"What makes sense Jasmine?" He said.

"A few months ago, she stopped talking and she because very clingy to me. It was all of a sudden. One day she was a talkative, playful little girl, then the next she was totally different. I didn't know what was wrong so I started taking her to counseling. I asked her if anyone had done anything to her and she said no. But she had gotten so clingy to me that she didn't want to have interactions with anyone other than me. It took quite a few visits to the counselor before she would even let me leave the room. Oh my God! Has he been doing this to her all this time?"* She broke down again.

"Jasmine I have to tell you something." Officer Steadman gave her time to calm down then continued, *"This isn't the first time he has done this. Your husband's real name is James Emmanuel Rollins, he's a registered sex offender and he's been to prison for molesting his then girlfriend's young daughter. He was sentenced to twenty five years but he was released on parole after serving only twelve."* He said.

Jasmine was stunned. She sat still just staring at the wall as tears rolled down her face. As Officer Steadman's words echoed in her head, she suddenly felt hot. Her whole body broke out in a sweat and she fainted. When she woke up, there was a cold towel on her head and an IV needle in her arm.

"How are you feeling?" The nurse asked.

"What happened? How did I get here?" Jasmine asked.

Before the nurse could answer, there was a knock at the door then Officer Roberts and Elaine Ferguson walked in. Jasmine wasn't in the mood to talk anymore but she knew that it was the only way to get her daughter back.

"Hi Jasmine. How are you feeling." Elaine asked.

"I'm okay." She said.

"I know that you're exhausted but I just wanted to give you an update on Camille." Elaine said.

Jasmine sat up on the bed.

"Well, we took her to one of our doctors who specializes in child molestation cases. She's very thorough and detailed when it comes to these types of cases and she was able to confirm that Camille had been molested. She took some swabs to be tested to make sure that she doesn't have any sexually transmitted diseases

and we'll have those results soon. Camille is currently in foster care where she'll stay until the investigation is over." Elaine said.

Jasmine sat staring at the wall. She didn't think that she couldn't cry anymore but the tears continued to fall. The only thing she could think about was Camille. She knew that her little girl had to be scared having her body examined and the thought of that broke her heart.

Chapter Eleven

Prior to going to the hospital to speak with Jasmine. Officer Roberts and Elaine Ferguson went to give Priscilla and update on the case but when they arrived to her office, she wasn't there.

"She's out for the rest of the day. Can I help you?" Amanda asked.

"It's very important that we speak to her today. Will you please call her? It's pertaining to the Camilla Rollins case and tell her that she may want to bring someone with her." Elaine said.

"Bring someone with her?" Amanda asked.

"Yes, we have some news that is going to upset her and she'll need all the support she can get." Elaine said.

Amanda had the ladies sit in the waiting area while she called Priscilla. She told her exactly what Elaine had said and Priscilla told her that she'd be right there.

Fifteen minutes later, Priscilla arrived, along with her mother Sheryl, her little sister, Tia, and her sister in law, Lori.

"Please follow me ladies. My husband and brother are on their way. We'll wait in my office until they arrive." Priscilla said. Her heart was beating so fast that it could be seen through her shirt.

By the time everyone was seated, Shawn, Kevin, and Pastor Rachel were walking through the door.

"Before we begin, do you mind if we have a moment of prayer?" Pastor Rachel said to Elaine.

Elaine nodded.

Dear God we come to you with our heads bowed and and our hearts leaning to you. As we gather here today, I'm asking that you fill this room with peace. Peace in our minds and in our hearts as we prepare to hear the news that was brought to us today. We also need strength so that we can handle whatever that news may be, Father. We ask all these things in your son Jesus' name. Amen...

Everyone sat down and looked in Elaine and Officer Ferguson's direction.

"I want to thank you for coming so quickly Priscilla. We both have some news to share with you and because of it's sensitivity, we wanted your support system here with you. Do you want to go first Elaine?" Office Ferguson said.

"Thanks Office Roberts. Although, due to privacy I'm unable to share a lot of information, I did want to tell you that Camilla is currently in foster care and due to the stress of everything, her mother is in the hospital. I don't know exactly what happened but I know that she was taken I for questioning and now she's at the hospital. We're going there right after we finish here." Elaine said.

Priscilla started crying. She was sitting between Pastor Rachel and Kevin. Both of them wrapped their arms around her.

"Priscilla, I know this is hard but I have some news as well and this is the reason that we needed your support system here. When Camilla's father was brought into the station, we did a background check on him while he was in questioning. He's been going by an Manny Rollins but his real name is James Emmanuel Rollins." Officer Roberts paused.

The room went silent. Everyone in the room, with the exception of Tia, knew exactly who he was.

"What?" Priscilla said.

"We found that once he was released from prison, he moved to California and altered his name. Within a years time, he had met and married Jasmine and when she became pregnant with

Camilla a few years later, he convinced her to move back here." Officer Roberts said.

"Excuse me." Shawn said then walked out the door. Lori went behind him.

"Shawn baby, I know you're upset but Priscilla needs you right now." Lori said. She had caught up with him and grabbed his arm. *"Come on baby. I know that this is hard but we all have to stay strong for Priscilla."*

"You don't understand. Okay Just let me go. I need a minute to be alone." He said and pulled away from her. Lori watched him walk away and as badly as she wanted to follow him, she decided to go back in with the family.

Shawn went outside and dialed Jasmine's phone number. It went to voicemail. *"Jasmine I need you to call me back as soon as possible."* He tried to call her again but again it went straight to voicemail. He paced back and forth trying to calm down. He couldn't believe what he had just heard. There was no way that all of that was a coincidence. He knew that all of this was about his daughter. The more he thought about it, he became more angry.

Damn it! He yelled.

Back in the office Pastor Rachel had her arms around Priscilla silently praying.

"So what's going to happen?" Sheryl asked.

"Well, we have enough evidence to arrest him so I'm pretty sure that charges will be filed no later than tomorrow." Officer Roberts explained.

"And our job is to protect the victim. Again, due to privacy I'm unable to share much but I will keep you posted Dr. Walton. We're going to leave now. We have to get to the hospital. Please give me a call if you have any questions." Elaine said.

"Here's my card. You can give me a call too." Officer Roberts said.

The two ladies left and for a while no one said anything. Sheryl held Tia, Kevin held Priscilla, and Pastor Rachel held Lori.

"Where did Shawn go?" Pastor Rachel asked.

"He needed some air. You know how protective he is when it comes to seeing any of us upset." Lori said.

Chapter Twelve

As Jasmine waited for the doctor to come in and release her, she sat on the edge of the hospital bed looking through her cellphone. The red light flashed signaling that she had more than thirty missed calls and even more text messages.

Before moving away from California to be with Manny, her family and friends warned her that she didn't know him well enough to just jump up and move across country.

"Baby I know that you're in love with him but are you sure you want to move so far away from your family, friends, and the only home you've ever known?" Her mother's words rand in her ears. Almost as if she were sitting in the room. Jasmine thought that her family didn't approve of Manny because he was black. She felt that they would never truly accept him or the biracial child she was carrying.

Manny promised that she would be happier and that his family would welcome her with opened arms.

It took a while for her to feel comfortable in the new city. She didn't know anyone other than Manny so she spent the first few months learning how to get around, finding doctors for her prenatal care, delivery, and a pediatrician for Camille once she was born.

She expected to meet his family as soon as they moved but that didn't happen until five months later. Manny explained that he had been disconnected from his family for awhile. He never told her why, he just said that it was a hurtful situation and he would tell her about it eventually.

Jasmine was very nervous meeting them for the first time. He had finally taken the initiative to make it happen and invited them over for dinner. The atmosphere was dense with tension. After being introduced and some small talk about where she was from,

Jasmine noticed that Manny barely had any interaction with his family.

"Congratulations on the new baby. Do you know what you're having yet?" His sister, Kelly asked.

"Yes it's a girl and we're so excited." Jasmine replied.

Manny's sister had a strange look on her face. Jasmine didn't quite know what it meant but the whole night was confusing. She didn't understand the silence and strange looks from Manny's family and he wasn't able to look anyone in the eyes.

"Good luck with delivery and if you need anything, please let us know." Kelly said.

Jasmine rubbed her belly and nodded. She couldn't tell if Kelly was sincere but she hoped so. Being in a new city with no friends or family was taking a toll on her. She had some days that she felt so lonely that she thought about moving back home but she couldn't imagine leaving Manny.

As the time neared that she would give birth to Camille, Manny's sister, Kelly did come around more. She came by at least three times a week to check on her and make sure she made it to her doctor's appointments. She even took her shopping for items for the baby.

"Since you're so new here, It would be a waste of time and money to throw you a baby shower. It would only be our family and it's fairly small but I will do what I can to help make sure my niece has everything she needs." Kelly said as she rubbed Jasmine's growing belly.

Kelly had really grown fond of Jasmine. As badly as she wanted to tell her to take her daughter and back home as fast as she could, she didn't. She simply prayed that her brother had truly changed as he said he did.

The Final Broken Piece   Beverly N. Vercher

*   *   *

When everything went down before, the family stood by him. He initially told them that it was all a lie and he never touched that little girl. Then when they got to court, it all changed. The evidence couldn't be denied but then he eventually broke down and confessed. The family felt betrayed and embarrassed. Kelly especially because she was the one who did an entire interview for the local news station proclaiming his innocence.

"I know my brother and if he says he didn't do it, I believe him. I don't know why this little girl would tell a story like this. She must be confused or someone must have told her to say it because I know my brother did not do this." **Kelly said during the interview.** She was already embarrassed but it seemed like every time the news came on, it showed the clip of that interview.

"I can't stay behind him for what he did. How can I visit him or give him money when he hurt that little girl like that? He'll get

out of prison and start a new life but that child will be scarred forever." Kelly said right after the trial when the family was altogether. *"You all can do what you want. I'm not telling you not to deal with him but I'm done. He's lied to me and embarrassed me. I just pray that God forgives me for calling that little girl and her mother a liar."*

For years, Kelly threw away the letters that her brother sent. She wouldn't even open them. Eventually he stopped writing. Then about six years later, she received another one and decided to open it. After reading the letter she worked on forgiving him by communicating often.

They wrote each other every week and her heart softened for him again. She always believed in second chances. *People can change.* She thought. At the time, she felt within her heart that he had really changed, she convinced him that moving to a differently city and state would be good for him. *"You don't need to stay around here where people will judge you and look at you crazy. If you're going to have any chance at getting a job and starting over, you have to move."* She said.

Kelly had a friend who moved to California after getting married. Her husband owned a construction company. She reached out to them for help with giving her brother a job and helping him find a place to stay. They agreed and the day after he was released from prison, he was on plane.

Chapter Thirteen

"Shawn, I know that you're upset with everything going on but baby please talk to me." Lori said from the other side of the door. Shawn had practically locked himself in his office for the past three days after they got the news about Priscilla's abuser. She knew that anytime something happened with his family, he took it very hard but this time it seems to be worse. He has never secluded himself from her. If anything they get closer.

"Baby I love you and I'm here when you're ready." She said sounding defeated.

As she made it to the end of the hall, she heard the door open and when she turned around, he was standing there. She went back and before entering the room he reached for her. For a few minutes they stood in one place just holding each other. He kissed her and when she felt the tears on his face, she instantly began to cry as well.

Shawn motioned for Lori to sit on the couch in his office and he sat beside her. His eyes were red so she could tell that he had to have been crying for quit some time.

She started to speak but he cut her off. *"No baby. Let me talk. First, I want to apologize for being so distant these past few days. I don't even know where to begin telling you what I'm going through right now but I'm going to try. I owe you that. I can't count the number of times I've asked God why he let this happen. I don't understand any of this and I've been trying to wrap my mind around it all but I can't and baby I need you."* He said.

"You're scaring me. What is it?" Lori said.

"All of this stuff with James. The man who abused my sister is much bigger than it looks. The little girl that he's in jail for now is my daughter. Camille is my daughter. I thought they still lived in California." He said.

"Wha...wha...what?" Lori said breathing heavily. It was like she had just been hit in the chest. *"Shawn, what are we going to do? Oh my God. I can't believe this. I'm at a loss for words right now."*

"I am too baby I don't know what to do but I think I need to tell my family first. Once I do that, we'll all be able to figure it out together. I just don't know how this will affect Priscilla. She's going through enough already." He said.

"Priscilla is hurting right now and I know that this news will hit her hard but she has to know. We'll make it through this and we'll do whatever it takes to get your daughter and keep her safe." She said.

*   *   *

A few days later, the entire family met at Shawn and Lori's home. He had personally paid each one a visit to invite them over because he had some important news to share and he wanted them all there to here it.

He visited Priscilla first.

"How are you doing?" He asked.

"Better." She said with a forced smile.

"No really, how are you doing Sis?" He said.

"I'm just taking one day at a time." She replied.

"Well, you don't have to worry about James. I'm telling you, if he comes anywhere near you, if he even calls you on the phone, he will have to deal with me." He said.

"Honestly Shawn, finding out that he was released from prison wasn't the thing that bothered me the most. It was what he did to that little girl. I remember the first day she walked in my office, I felt a connection with her. Something about her reminded me of me but never in a million years would I have thought that she was

being molested by the same man, who is her father, that did it to me, so many years ago." She said as she fought the tears welling in her eyes.

Shawn hugged her. *"Everything is going to be alright sis. We've gone through a lot since we were children but we're strong and we can make it through anything."*

"You're right." She replied.

"I have to go but I'll see you tomorrow. Make sure you all be there by seven o'clock. Lori is cooking dinner." He said.

"Okay brother. We'll be there." She said.

Normally Priscilla would be curious about Shawn and Lori's news and would try to pry it out of him but she's so mentally and emotionally drained that she couldn't process anything else at the moment.

*   *   *

Shawn's next stop was to see Sheryl. When he arrived, Sheryl told him that Malcolm and Tiana had gone to the store.

"I can't promise that they'll be back before you leave. They actually went to the grocery store and they have to go up and down each and every isle. That's why I chose to stay home. But, is everything okay with you and Lori?" Sheryl asked.

"Yes, we're okay Mama. We just want to tell everyone all at the same time and answer any questions." He replied.

"Now I'm going to be worried and anxious all night. Can you give me a hint?" She asked.

"No ma'am. Tomorrow will be here before you know it." He said smiling.

"Well, at least you're smiling so I guess it's good news." She said. He hugged her and gave her a kiss on the forehead.

"I'll see you tomorrow and tell Malcolm and Tiana that I said hello." He said.

*   *   *

He saved his grandparents for last. He knew that they would have counseling and prayer like always.

"I can't go into it right now Nana. Lori and I want everyone there at the same time so that we can answer all of your questions." Shawn said after Pastor Rachel tried to convince him to tell her the news.

"I just pray that whatever it is, it's part of God's plan." She said.

"Trust me. We've prayed about it and I've talked to God more lately than I ever have." He replied.

After a long prayer, Shawn left.

Chapter Fourteen

"Mrs. Rollins, I know that you've been through a lot over the past week. I want to assure you that Camille is doing well. You'll be able to see her as soon as the investigation is complete. I'm just here to ask you a few more questions. A few days ago, we were contacted by a Mr. Shawn Jones. Can you tell me who that is?" Elaine Ferguson said.

Jasmine put her face in her hands.

"Mrs. Rollins?" Elaine said.

"It's Camille's biological father." Jasmine said.

"Mrs. Rollins, so are you telling me that Mr. Rollins isn't her father? Does he know that?" Elaine asked.

"No he's not aware that Camille is not his biological daughter. We were having problems earlier in our marriage and during that time, I met Shawn; he was in California on assignment with the

military and for the few months that he was there, we were seeing each other. When I found out that I was pregnant, I told Shawn. And when she was born, we had a DNA test and when she came back his, we agreed that, for the sake of both our marriages, we would keep it a secret and let Manny raise her as his own. We agreed on child support and he sends me a bank transfer every month. Manny never knew any of this. When did Shawn contact you? How does he even know about this? He's been calling me and leaving me messages but I never answered." Jasmine replied.

Elaine sat quietly as Jasmine shared this secret with her. She knew that it was the truth because, Shawn's story was similar.

"Well, I just want you to know that this situation has grown to be quite complexing and I'm sure he'll want to get involved in some way so be prepared." Elaine said.

Jasmine was silent. Actually speechless. *How did he find out?* She thought to herself.

"You need to sit down so that I can share the rest of this with you." Elaine said.

Jasmine sat down slowly and asked, *"What else could there be?"*

"There's definitely more. As you were told previously, Mr. Rollins has been to prison for molesting a child before and that child was Dr. Walton. He was dating her mother at the time and back then the laws were a little different. They couldn't believe that something like this could happen without the mother knowing so they were going to convict their mother too. And the stress was too much for her so she committed suicide." Elaine said.

Jasmine sat quietly in shock. She tried to speak but she couldn't find any words to say. She was just waiting to wake up from this nightmare.

"Mrs. Rollins are you okay?" Elaine asked.

Jasmine continued to stare into space. Her mind was in a state of confusion. Then the room started turning dark.

*   *   *

James had been in jail for more than a week a no one other than his lawyer had come to see him. He reached out to his family but when he told them why he was in jail they all told him never to contact them again. They wouldn't stand behind him a second time.

"I know that I'm sick. I need help. I can't do this alone. Please don't turn your back on me." He begged to his sister. She didn't reply. She just hung up.

James had stopped eating and grooming himself. His untamed facial hair and weight loss made him look much older. In the short amount of time, he had already loss so much weight that his face was visibly thinner and his clothes were fitting very loose.

"Have you started eating?" Attorney Morrison asked.

Manny shook his head.

"You need to eat. You'll need your strength to make it through the trial. There are some things that have come up that I must make you aware of. Are you listening." Attorney Morrison asked.

James nodded while looking down at his feet.

"Look at me. I need to know that you understand what I'm about to tell you." Attorney Morrison said.

James finally raised his head.

"Did you ever go to any of Camille's counseling sessions?" Attorney Morrison asked.

"No why?" James replied.

Attorney Morrison let out a deep breath and loosened his tie.

"Camille's counselor's name was Priscilla Walton, maiden name, Priscilla Jones." Attorney Morrison said.

"What did you just say?" James replied.

"You heard me correctly and there's more. A man heard about the case and decided to come forward and claim that he's Camille's biological father. Apparently he and Jasmine had an affair. They also had a DNA test and it proved that he's her father. He's been sending her money every month since then." Attorney Morrison said.

James tried to stand up but the police guard that was in the room said, *"Stay in your seat Mr. Rollins."*

"So you mean to tell me that Camille is not my daughter and Jasmine has been lying to me all these years?" James asked.

"None of that matters when it comes to your case. I just wanted to let you know all the details of what's going on right now." Attorney Morrison said.

James stared at Attorney Morrison. He looked as is he was waiting for Attorney Morrison to say that he's just joking.

"I know that this is shocking I was flabbergasted when I got this information. I reviewed your old case with Priscilla and saw that she kept a notebook." Attorney Morrison said.

James nodded.

"Well, she told Camille to do that and a coloring book was found. They also found two pair of her panties that tested positive for your DNA. You told me that you never actually penetrated her. Well, if you didn't how did that get there. I can't help you if you lie to me." Attorney Morrison said almost yelling.

"I'm not going to deny that I'm sick and that I hurt my daughter..Camille. But I never penetrated her. It must of got there when I...finished up." James said. His voice was quivering. Saying what he did out loud made him feel sick to his stomach.

"Okay, I have to be honest with you. This is going to be hard but I will fight for you." Attorney Morrison replied.

"At this point, I have nothing to lose. I've lost my family, my wife, and my daughter. I'm going to plead guilty and accept whatever the judge gives me. Maybe I do need to be locked up forever." James said.

"You don't want to go to prison for the rest of your life James. Pleading guilty and showing them how remorseful you are will look good and maybe we can get the judge to see that you need help. Just to be clear, you're not getting less than twenty years but I'm hoping that after you serve ten to fifteen years, you can be released to a facility to get counseling" Attorney Morrison said.

"I had counseling before. When I got out of prison, I thought I was cured. I met Jasmine and she and I had a great sexual relationship. I was totally attracted to her which is different than before. The desire didn't come back until a year ago and I just couldn't help myself. It's like something inside me takes over and I have no control." James replied.

"James, I just need you to eat and take care of yourself as best you can. This is going to be hard and you will need your strength. I'll come back to see you next week. I should have another update by then." Attorney Morrison said.

Chapter Fifteen

Shawn was up before dawn the next day. His anxiety was at an all time high. Every time he practiced what he was going to say, the words seemed to escape his mind. He was grateful to still have Lori. She always knew what to say. She was good at speaking to people and having difficult conversations while remaining calm. The thing that worried him the most was the effect all of this will have on Priscilla. She was already going through so much but as badly as he wanted to avoid this situation, he couldn't. For the sake of his daughter, he had to do this.

He sat in his office, looking at the photo of her that he had hidden in the file cabinet, and thought about how adamant he was about not being in Camille's life. For the first time, he cried for her. *If I had been there, this wouldn't have happened to you.* He said then kissed the picture.

*　　　*　　　*

Lori wasn't surprised when she woke up and found that Shawn had already locked himself in his office. It was his refuge. The place he went to clear his mind.

She went to the kitchen to prepare breakfast for them. *It's going to be a stressful day. We need a good breakfast,* she said out loud as she looked hat her reflection in her favorite stainless steel frying pan.

The smell of bacon frying never fails at getting Shawn to come out of his office and shortly after adding the bacon to the frying pan, Shawn wrapped his arms around her from behind. Lori loved when he did that. Many times they wouldn't say a word. She would continue to cook as he held her and kissed her neck. Those intimate moments reminded her of the love they shared for each other.

"Hey you. How are you feeling?" She asked.

"I'm okay. Just ready to get this over with." He replied.

"I know but it's going to be alright. Your family loves you and although this is going to be a shock to them, they'll still love you and I will too." She said.

"You're right but my main concern is Priscilla. I'm not sure how she's going to take all of this but I can't not tell her. She has to know that Camille is her niece and she needs her." He said.

"I must admit that it will be hard but we'll get through it. I prayed about it and I know that God is going to work it all out." Lori said.

Shawn poured him and Lori a cup of coffee and went to the table. She shortly followed with their plates.

*"I don't think I tell you how much I love and appreciate you enough. Baby you mean the world to me and I'm so sorry for the

mistakes. I love you with all my heart and I appreciate you for sticking by me through all the pain I've caused." Shawn said.

Lori held him. *"I would never let you go through this alone."*

After breakfast Lori went to take a shower and Shawn went back to his office. He sat as his desk staring at the photo of Camille. He never realized that he could love her so much. When he found out that he was her biological father, he was devastated. Selfishly he could only think about himself and how he could hide her from his wife and family. He's consumed with regret and grief because he failed to protect the who should be the most important person in his life.

God it's been a minute. Other than praying with my wife and family, you haven't heard directly from me in a while. I'm sorry. Please forgive me . I need you Lord. I need you to grant me the strength and insight that I need on the hard journey that I have embarked on. I know that I don't deserve Camille after how I treated her but God you know that she deserves us. She needs a

family that will love and protect her. I failed at that once but I promise you God that it will never happen again. Please help me, Lori, the rest of my family, especially Priscilla. We're going to need you more than ever. Thank you for your grace, mercy, and forgiveness. In Jesus name, Amen.

He dried his tears and sat quietly with his eyes closed. A few moments later, Lori tapped on the door to let him know that she was out of the shower.

"Okay honey. I'll be out in a few." He said.

She smiled and closed he door. H would need two reminders before he actually went to take a shower.

Lori looked at the clock and realized that everyone would start arriving in about six hours which gave her plenty of time to go grocery shopping and prepare dinner.

*　　　　　*　　　　　*

"Hey, I just pulled up at the house. I need help with the bags." Lori said.

A few seconds later, Shawn would come through the door.

"You're planning to cook a feast, huh?" He said; smiling.

"Good food always makes people feel better." She said.

"Do you need help with anything?" He asked.

"Nope. I got this." She replied.

Shawn pulled Lori close to him and kissed her. *"I'll be in my office if you need me."*

Lori always loved to cook and she was very excited to receive a recipe box from Pastor Rachel. Not only did she include some of Shawn's favorites but Priscilla's and Sheryl's as well.

"Since you love to cook, I want you to be able to make their favorite foods just like I do." Pastor Rachel said as she handed the box to Lori.

It was the most meaningful gift Lori has ever received and she promised to cherish it forever.

*   *   *

Shawn sat in his office again, staring at Camille's photo. He had so many thoughts going through his head that it was hard to keep them straight.

He planned to speak to the department of social services about how to go about getting custody of Camille and he planned to visit Jasmine. He prayed that she wouldn't fight him and although he felt that she had every right to be angry with him, Shawn hoped that she would simply keep Camille's best interest in mind.

He turned around in his chair so that he could look out of the window and he imagined him and Camille playing in the backyard. He held the photo of Camille up and said *I can't wait.*

*　　　*　　　*

"Hey you." Shawn said as he peeked around the kitchen corner.

"Hey what's up?" Lori said. She didn't even look up. She just continued chopping onions.

"Nothing. I was thinking that I spend so much time secluded in my office. I know that sometimes you've felt ignored and neglected and I want to apologize for that. I want to be more present for you so I promise to spend less time in there." He said.

"Thanks Baby. I really appreciate that but you don't have to start right now." She said.

Shawn knew that his wife liked to be alone when she's cooking a large meal so he kissed her on the cheek and went to sit on the back porch to get some fresh air and to think.

Chapter Sixteen

Jasmine really looked forward to her counseling appointments each week. The grief of what happened to Camille was still hard for her to bear. She even tried reaching out to her mother but her call went unanswered again. Her own family had no idea what was going on in her life that that made her feel even worse. After all the years that have passed, she truly missed her family. She actually wanted to hear them say, *I told you so,* just to be able to talk to them.

Going through the trauma alone made the situation even harder for her but her counseling sessions helped her get through the week. It gave her something to look forward to.

She was referred to a therapist by the department of social services but she decided to seek her own. She wasn't too sure how well she could trust that they would truly give her the help that she needs or just collect information to use against her. So she googled therapists in the area and after reading the reviews, she called, Dr. Catrina Bell. She was highly recommended and had all five star reviews

"So Mrs. Rollins, how are you today?" Dr. Bell asked.

"Exhausted." Jasmine replied.

"Please explain." Dr. Bell said.

"I still haven't slept much and when I do, I have terrible nightmares about what happened to Camille. I miss my baby so much." Jasmine said.

"Did you do the exercises?" Dr. Bell asked.

"I tried but most days, I just lay in bed." Jasmine replied.

Dr. Bell told Jasmine to meditate daily. She provided her with all information and techniques to meditate.

"Meditation is vital in easing stress. You're able to take a few moments to clear your mind and with deep breathing, you can slow your heart rate down and lower your blood pressure." Dr. Bell said at the previous session.

"I will try to do it more but honestly, it takes every bit of energy that I have to just get out of bed and take a shower everyday." Jasmine said.

"I understand but the meditation will really help you deal with all of the emotions. Starting tomorrow, try doing it as soon as you get up. When you muster up the strength to get out of bed, immediately start meditating then drink a tall glass of water." Dr. Bell said.

"Okay I'll try." Jasmine said.

"So talk to me about what's been going through your mind about your daughter and the upcoming court hearing for your husband." Dr. Bell asked.

"That has really been hard to think about. Like I said, I miss my baby. She should be with me, not strangers. And I'm just ready to go to court and see Manny go to prison." Jasmine replied.

"Are you prepared to hear all the details of what he did to your daughter? You have to get prepared for that Jasmine." Dr. Bell said.

Jasmine put her face in her hands. The thought of what happened to Camille was heartbreaking.

"Honestly, Dr. Bell, I don't think I'll ever be ready for that. Just thinking about it brings me to tears so I'm not sure how I'm going to make it through actually hearing it first hand." Jasmine said.

"My job is to help you learn to deal with all of this and coping with the emotions in a healthy way. I know that this will be hard for you but I need you to fight.

Not just for yourself but for your daughter. She needs a strong woman to stand up for her and the court needs to see that you'll do anything to protect your child. You can't just sit back an wallow in your pain. Use it as fuel to fight." Dr. Bell said.

* * *

Jasmine always left her therapy sessions feeling so much better but as soon as she got back to her empty house, the cloud of depression would take over. She missed the sound of Camille playing with her toys. She even missed cooking for her and getting her ready for school. The toys she was playing with last were still in the living room floor.

Her cellphone rung, snapping her the thought. When she saw Shawn's number on the screen, she ignored the call again. He had called her several times since the incident but she wasn't ready to deal with him just yet. She knew that eventually she would have to talk to him but her main focus was getting her daughter back.

She pressed the ignore button and headed to her bed room where she spent most of her time. She changed into her pajamas and got in bed. The tv was on but, as always, it was watching her more than she watched it.

A few moments later, she dosed off only to be awakened by her phone ringing again. She didn't recognize the number but with so many calls from case workers, she couldn't afford not to answer.

"Hello." She said.

"Hi mommy." Camille's voice said through the phone.

Jasmine immediately sat up on her bed.

"Camille is that you?" Oh my God baby. Is that you?" Jasmine asked.

"Yes mommy. I miss you. When are you coming to get me?" Camille said.

"Soon baby I swear. Are you okay? Have they been nice to you?" Jasmine said.

"Yes mommy. They are nice to me but I miss you. I'm ready to go home." Camille said.

Tears were already streaming down Jasmine's face and when she heard her daughter's cry, she almost broke down. She remembered that Dr. Bell said she needed to be strong for her daughter.

They talked a few minutes longer then Jasmine heard the case worker tell Camille to say goodbye and she promised that she could call again soon.

"Hi Mrs. Rollins. My name is Andrea Shoals, I am the case worker assigned to Camille's care. I check in with her twice a week and accompany her to all of her counseling sessions. I want you to know that she's doing great. That's why I thought it would be a good idea to let her talk to you." Andrea said.

"Thank you so much for letting her call me. It meant to world to me to hear her voice. I've missed her so much." Jasmine said.

"You're welcome. I did it for her because she's asked for you many times. I'll be in touch again soon. Goodbye." Andrea said then ended the call.

Jasmine let out the scream that built up in her chest. Finally hearing her daughter's voice was music to her ears but it made her miss her even more.

God, I just want my baby back. Please show me a sign. What should I do? I'll do anything just to have her back with me.

Please forgive me for all my sins that lead to this happening. God please forgive me for the affair and all the other things I've done to hurt you. Please just give me my baby back and I'll do whatever you want me to do.

A few moments later, her phone rung again and it was Shawn.

She looked to the sky wondering if this was a sign from God. For the sake of her daughter she answered.

"Hello." Jasmine said.

"Hi Jasmine. I'm glad you finally answered. I'm sure you know by now that I know what's going on with Camille and I want to help." Shawn said.

Jasmine was quiet.

"Hello, Jasmine, are you there?" Shawn asked.

"Yes I'm here. I just don't know what to say. What about your wife? The reason that you didn't want anything to do with

Camille was because you didn't want to ruin your marriage. Now you're calling out the blue to help. Help how Shawn? Do you think she won't find out?" She said.

"Jasmine, she already knows and she wants to help as well.

Camille needs me and if you let me, I want to be there. I'm sorry for everything that happened before and I'm sorry for neglecting her, and hurting you but she needs me now and that's all that matters to right now." He said.

Chapter Seventeen

As expected, Sheryl, Tia, and Pastor Rachel arrived first. When there was a family gathering of any sort, you could always count on them to be early. Tia jumped out of the car and ran when she saw Shawn standing on the front porch. She was always excited to see her siblings. Especially Shawn because she doesn't get to see him as often as she does Priscilla.

"Hey you." He said then kissed her on the forehead.

"Hey big brother. I missed you!" Tia said hugging him as tight as she could.

"I missed you too baby girl. We have to spend more time together. You're growing up too fast on me." He said.

"Hey Mama. Hey Nana. Thank you for coming." Shawn said as he greeted Sheryl and Pastor Rachel.

He hugged them then opened to door for them to enter the house.

"It sure does smell good in here. Lori is doing some serious cooking today." Pastor Rachel said as she entered the kitchen.

"Only with the help of your amazing recipes." Lori said.

"Do you need any help baby?" Pastor Rachel asked. Lori liked being in the kitchen alone but she knew better than to say no.

"Yes ma'am. If you don't mind. I would love for you to make your famous mashed potatoes. I just got the potatoes out of the oven." Lori said.

"You see, baking is the secret to good mashed potatoes. Seasoning, smothering them in butter, then putting them in the oven makes them so much more flavorful." Pastor Rachel said as she washed her hands.

A few minutes later, Shawn and Sheryl entered the kitchen.

"Lori, you put my grandmother to work and she's a guest?" He laughed knowing good and well that Pastor Rachel would have

prepared the whole meal if asked.

"Do you need me to help." Sheryl asked.

"Go on honey, we got this." Pastor Rachel said.

"Do you want to join me on the porch mom? It's nice out there." Shawn asked.

"Tia, your brother and I will be on the porch. Stay out of your sister in law and grandmother's way." Sheryl said as Tia came out of the bathroom.

"If you want, you can go downstairs. We've finally finished the basement so there's a tv, stereo, and everything down there." Lori said.

Tia's eyes brightened. *"Thank you Lori!"* she said and hurried to the door at the end of the hallway.

Shawn and Sheryl made themselves comfortable outside as they waited for Priscilla and her family to arrive.

"Shawn, I must admit that I'm a little concerned about this meeting. What's the big secret? Why did you have to wait until we were altogether to tell us?" Sheryl asked.

"Mama, to be honest. This will not be the easiest meeting for us. The news that I have to share is going to be shocking to all of you but I've been keeping this secret for too long. Our lives are going to change but I'm hoping that it will change for the better." Shawn said.

By the look on Sheryl's face, he knew that he had only worried her more but he had to be honest with her.

    *   *   *

Priscilla arrived right on time. Shawn looked at his watch and smiled. She was always on time. Never early and never late.

"Hey Nana, hey uncle Shawn!" Priscilla's kids yelled out of the car window then the door burst open and all three little ones ran to hug Sheryl first then Shawn.

"Hi mom. Hi brother." Priscilla said then hugged them.

"What's up brother in law." Priscilla's husband, Kevin, said as he and Shawn hugged.

"How are you feeling today, baby." Sheryl asked Priscilla.

"I feel better. I'm just happy to be here with all of my family. I've been really looking forward to this." Priscilla said.

Sheryl hugged her and they all went into the house.

By the time everyone greeted each other, Lori was pulling the pan of dinner rolls out of the oven. They all knew that meant dinner was ready.

Tia, Shemar, Dominic, and Shay, had the task of setting the table and when they were done, Lori, Pastor Rachel, and Shawn brought all the food out.

The spread on the table was almost like Thanksgiving dinner.

"This looks great Lori. Everything looks and smells amazing." Priscilla said.

"Thanks to Mama Rachel for her recipes and her help today." Lori replied.

"Oh baby, you already had it going on way before I got here." Pastor Rachel said.

*   *   *

As soon as dinner was done and the table was clear, Tia and Priscilla's kids went downstairs. Sheryl had asked Tia, prior to them arriving, if she would look after her niece and nephews while they talked.

All of the adults went to the living room and suddenly the mood changed. Although no one knew what this important meeting was about, they knew that it was something serious. Shawn and Lori's demeanor didn't seem joyful so they all knew that it was a serious issue.

Chapter Eighteen

"I'm sorry Mr. Rollins. If we had caught this earlier, we may have been able to do something. But unfortunately, you're already in Stage 4 so Chemo won't even work. We can only give you medications that will help make you comfortable." The doctor said.

Manny finally went to the doctor after he started coughing up blood. He'd been experiencing sharp pains in his stomach off and on for more that a year but he never made it a point to go to the doctor. Since the pains weren't constant he didn't think it was anything serious.

As he sat there and listened to the doctor tell him that he has Stage 4 Stomach Cancer, made him speechless. He was torn between being afraid and feelings as if he deserved to die like this.

"How long do I have?" He asked.

"If you have any affairs to get in order, you need to do it soon. Based on the results of your second MRI, you have about three months and the last thirty days will leave you bed ridden. This is an aggressive cancer so it's going to move hard and fast." He replied.

Manny's heart sank. He sat quietly as he listened to the doctor give him instructions on how to live out his final days.

The words *Get your affairs in order,* continued to echo through his mind on the walk back to his cell. As badly as he wanted to call his family, he knew that they wouldn't answer and Jasmine was out of the question. He didn't have any friends or anyone else that he could think of that might care that he's dying.

He sat on his bed thinking long into the night. He stayed in the same position, staring into space, even after lights out.

The Final Broken Piece   Beverly N. Vercher

* * *

Manny forced himself to eat a few bites of breakfast. His appetite had been almost non existent for the past few months. He thought it was the guilt of what he had done but at that time, he realized that the cancer must have had a lot to do with it.

Back in his cell, he fought back tears as he thought of the fact that he would die alone in prison. When he was incarcerated before, he saw the burial ground of all the unclaimed prisoners that died while locked up. They had no family or friends to give them a proper burial and it saddened Manny and now he's facing the same fate.

Although he knew that it probably wouldn't change anything, he decided to write a letter to everyone he had hurt. He wasn't doing it to gain forgiveness from them but to free himself of all the lies, secrets, and shame in hopes that God will forgive him.

The Final Broken Piece   Beverly N. Vercher

I may die alone but God I hope that you will still forgive me. He whispered as he looked up to the sky.

*   *   *

Dear Jasmine,

I know that I'm the last person that you want to hear from and I wouldn't be surprised if you never ever read this letter. But in the case that you do, I just want to say I'm sorry. I know that it sounds to simple compared to what I've done to you and especially Camille but when I try to think of something more, the words escape me. I'm a sick man, not just physically but mentally as well and I'm not using that as an excuse for what I did but it's the truth. I thought I was healed when I was released from prison. I hadn't felt that kind of desire in so long and I thought I was cured. It's a sickness that started when I was a child myself. It happened to me so it turned me into this monster. Again, not an excuse, I just want you to understand. None of this is your fault. There is no way you would have known who I was. I did everything I could to hide it; even changed my name so that if someone had looked me up, they wouldn't have found out the truth. I hope that you're able to get Camille back soon so that the two of you can start the healing process. I'm not even asking for your forgiveness because I don't deserve it. I will get exactly what I deserve; prison and death and I'm prepared for both.

Please know that the love I have for you is real. I've always loved you and Camille with all my heart. Even with all the lies and the pain, my love was true.

Goodbye Jasmine.

Love you, Manny

He put the letter in an envelope, wrote her name and address on it, sat it to the side, and started on the next one.

Dear Kelly,

You asked me never to contact you again, I needed to for the last time. Baby sister, I know that I've hurt you, disappointed you, and embarrassed you. You are the best sister anyone could have and I took advantage of your love and loyalty to me and I'm writing to apologize for that.

I'm reflecting on our lives and everything we've been through and not matter what, I've always known that I had you if no one else. I should have told you what happened to me along time ago, then maybe you would understand this sickness I have. There is no excuse for my actions, I don't deserve your forgiveness, and I deserve everything that is about to happen to me.

I will die in prison alone. I've been diagnosed with Stage 4 Stomach Cancer and I only have about three months to live.

The Final Broken Piece   Beverly N. Vercher

I have come to terms with death because I feel that it's what I deserve. All the pain that I've caused to my victims and their families is unforgivable and maybe God felt that death is the only punishment that I deserve. If that's the case, I agree.

I just want to thank you for everything you've ever done for me. Although you're my little sister, you've always taken care of me instead of me taking care of you and I appreciate it all. I pray that once I'm gone, you'll be able to forget about me and move on with your life. I wish you nothing but joy and happiness.

I love you and I'm sorry.

Love, James.

Chapter Nineteen,

Shawn looked around the room at his family. He could see the concern in their faces and it made his heart sink. Lori stood beside him and held his hand. That calmed his racing heart a little.

"Lori and I invited you all here today to share something with you. I want to first say that I'm sorry for making you all wait but I wanted to tell all of you at one time. This isn't easy for me. I know that I will disappoint you but I hope that all of you will forgive me. I've prayed about it and I know that I'm doing the right thing, I just need to know that I'll have the support of my family." Shawn said.

"Go on baby. You're doing good." Lori whispered.

"Okay. I have a daughter." He said and paused.

"What?" Priscilla acted surprised. She didn't want Shawn to know that Lori had already told her.

"Oh my goodness." Cheryl said.

"There's more. She's the result of an affair a had years ago. Her mother was married as well so we decided to keep it a secret and other than the monthly payment that I sent her, the husband would raise the child as his own. I never wanted or even tried to have a relationship with the child. I was selfish and I regret that every day now. Her name is Camille and she's seven years old." He said and paused again.

Priscilla had a horrified look on her face. She walked closer to Shawn and asked, *"Brother, are you telling me that she is your daughter? The little girl that..."*

"Yes. She's your niece." He replied.

Priscilla began to cry. Shawn held her in his arms and tears started to run down his face as well. The entire family joined them in a group hug and wept together as Pastor Rachel began to pray.

Dear God,

We need you. We need you Father. Now more than ever. We need your strength and your guidance. Please wrap your arms around this family and bring peace to this room and peace to our hearts. We need you Father. Father we need you...

In Jesus' name...Amen

She grabbed the box of tissues, wiped the tears from her own eyes, then started passing them out. When everyone was seated Lori began to speak.

"I know that this is a shock for all of you. For the past few weeks, Shawn and I have prayed and talked to God probably more than we ever have. We had to work through the situation but I've totally forgiven him and will continue to stay by his side as his wife. Our main focus right now is helping Camille and Jasmine in

any way that we can. Shawn has spoken in Jasmine and right now, as you can imagine, she's going through a lot emotionally. Camille is still in foster care and she is alone dealing with the fact that her husband molested her daughter. Our goal isn't to take Camille from her but to build a loving relationship with her as she gets to know us. She needs to know that she has a family that loves her because that will be so vital on her journey to healing. Priscilla I remember you telling me that your family was your strength as you went through the healing process so I know that Camille will make it through just like you did but she needs all of us." She said.

The room was quiet. Shawn and Lori wanted to let it all soak in before saying else.

"You're right Lori. Having a loving, supportive, and praying family helped me through the darkest hours of my life. It's just so

crazy that the very first time I met with Camille, I said to myself that she reminded me so much of me and that connection is how I was able to figure out what was happening to her. Oh my God, she's my niece." Priscilla said.

"Shawn, why didn't you tell us? You know we would have welcomed her with opened arms." Cheryl asked.

"Mama, I was ashamed and afraid. Afraid to lose Lori and ashamed that I had messed up so badly that I would disappoint all of you. I want to apologize to my wife again and to all of you for not sharing this with you. There is no excuse for denying a child of her father's love but I promised God that if he allows me to, I'll grab on to her and never let her go. All I have is a photo of her and I look at it every day. I've fallen in love with her like a father is supposed to love his daughter and I just need for her to be alright." Shawn said and for the first time, he broke down. He

fell to his knees and sobbed. His family embraced him just as they did Priscilla.

"Shawn it's okay. We forgive you and most importantly, God has forgiven you too. You just let us know what we need to do." Pastor Rachel said.

"Yes son, we're here for you." Cheryl said.

"She's my niece and something inside me already knew it. Brother, you know that I'm here for you. I have to get in touch with my contact at the department of social services to see how we need to proceed further. I don't want to jeopardize the case in any way by being involved since I was her therapist. I'm not sure how that will work but I'll find out. No matter what, I'm here." Priscilla said.

"All of this has weighed heavy on my heart and now that I've told all of you, I feel so much better." Shawn said.

They all sat around and talked about Camille and how excited they were to welcome her into the family. They all agreed that including Jasmine would be a good idea as well. Camille needed a solid support system and that included her mother.

*   *   *

When everyone left, Lori and Shawn sat at the kitchen table having a cup of tea.

"Baby, I just want to say thank you again. You are the best thing that ever happened to me and I thank God everyday for allowing me to share my life with you." Shawn said as he looked into Lori's eyes.

She fought back the tears and replied, *"You don't have to keep apologizing or thanking me. Shawn, I love you and I forgave you a long time ago. I'm just ready to bring Camille in and love her as if I gave birth to her myself."*

He leaned across the table, kissed her, and said, *"I'm going to take a shower. You should join me."*

She smiled. The intimate side of their marriage had taken a back seat to everything that was going on and she was excited to make love to her husband that night.

Chapter Twenty

The sound of her cellphone ringing startled Jasmine out of her sleep.

"Hello", she said with a raspy voice.

"Hi. Mrs. Rollins. It's Andrea Shoals, Camille's case worker. How are you?" she said.

"I'm fine. Is Camille okay?" Jasmine asked.

"Yes, yes she's fine. I'm calling because you've been authorized a visit with her so I want to set that up as soon as possible. She's going to be so excited to see you." Andrea replied.

"Oh my goodness. You don't know how happy I am." Jasmine said. Tears were rolling down her face. She looked up to the sky and said, *"Thank you God."*

*"Camille has asked for you everyday and normally she has a

pleasant demeanor but for the past few days she's been withdrawn and not very interactive with her foster parents or the children. So, I spoke to my supervisor about it and she thought that it may be a good idea to let you visit this one time. But if it goes well, we will definitely try to get more visits for the two of you." Andrea said.

*   *   *

The visit was scheduled at her home the following day and Jasmine hardly slept at all the night before. She had cleaned the house top to bottom so it was spotless. The investigators had stripped everything of Camille's bed for evidence so Jasmine went and bought new bedding and a few new toys for her.

To her surprise, Shawn continued to send her the money. She thought it would stop since he knew that Camille wasn't in her custody. She still wasn't sure how she was going to handle him or his wife but that was the late thing on her list that day. She just wanted to hug her baby again.

The clock seeming to be going backwards. Camille was scheduled to arrive at three o'clock and Jasmine could have sworn that when she looked at the clock an hour ago it was one fifteen. *Why is it only one forty two?* She said out loud

She checked her phone and every clock in the house just to make sure the time was right. She tried to watch tv and read but nothing worked. She felt herself getting frustrated so she decided to take a hot bath to calm her nerves.

The hot water and lavender bubbles surrounded her body like a blanket. She slid down in the water, closed her eyes, and relaxed her body. Within minutes, she felt a little better.

The bath helped time go by a little faster for her. By the time she got out of the tub, got dressed, and did her hair, it was almost three o'clock.

She went to the living room and peeked out the window. She was so excited that she almost wanted to sit on the porch and wait for them. She continued to look out the window and a few moments later, she saw a blue Ford Fusion pulling in her driveway. Her heart was racing and she tried to resist the urge to run outside but she couldn't. By the time she made it down the stairs, the back door of the car swung open and Camille jumped out.

"Mommy!" Camille yelled as she ran to her mother's arms.

Jasmine stooped down and embraced her. *"My baby. I've missed you so much."* She said as she smothered her daughter with kisses.

Jasmine picked her daughter up and they all went in the house.

"Would you like something to drink?" Jasmine asked.

Andrea said, *"No."*

"I made lemonade." Jasmine said smiling at Camille. She knew that it was her daughter's favorite.

"Ooh yes mommy!" She said.

"I have a surprise for you too. I redecorated your whole room!" Jasmine said. Camille didn't look as excited as she had hoped but she understood. *"Hey, I know that you've been through a lot and I'm so sorry but I promise that I will never let any hurt you again. You'll be home soon and we're going to start over. Okay? A fresh new start. Just you and me."* Camille hugged her so tightly that she could feel her little heart beating through her chest. It took all the strength she had to fight back the tears.

"I love you mommy." Camille whispered.

After finishing her lemonade, Jasmine lead her to her room. Her eyes lit up when she saw how bright and colorful her room was. All of the furniture was rearranged and it looked like a totally different room. You can play in here while Ms. Shoals and I talk.

"Okay." Camille said without even looking up. She was already playing with the new doll that was laying on her bed.

Andrea noticed the smile on Jasmine's face. She's been trained to keep her emotions out of it but sometimes she couldn't help it. She loved seeing parents and children placed back together.

"I just want to thank you for this visit. I've really missed my baby." Camille said.

"I can tell and she has missed you too. I think this is good for her I explained to her that she can't stay today but I know it's still going to be hard when it's time to go." Andrea said.

"It's going to be hard for me too but I'm praying that I'll see her again soon and I'm praying that she'll come home for good soon too. Do you have any idea when that will be?" Jasmine said.

"That will be determined by and judge. You should be getting a letter confirming the date of your hearing soon. I really don't have any additional information to add. I'm sorry." Andrea said. She knew more but she couldn't share it with Jasmine.

"Alright, I'll be on the lookout for it. I'm just ready for all of this to be over." Jasmine said.

"What about the court date for your husband? Have you gotten that information yet?" Andrea ask

Jasmine hated to hear him referred to as her husband. *"Yes it's next month on the seventeenth at nine am."*

"Okay good. I know that you're nervous and anxious but you won't have to go alone. I'll be there with you for support." Andrea said.

"Thank you, I appreciate that. I'll need all the support I can get." Jasmine said.

The ladies talked a few more minutes then Andrea announced that the visit was coming to an end. Jasmine called Camille to reassure her that they will be together again. It was hard seeing her go again. They both cried.

Andrea promised Camille that she would let her call her mother in a few days and they would visit again soon as well.

Jasmine stood on the porch and watched the car back out of the driveway. She stood there and watched them go up the street until they disappeared around the corner. She used the sleeve of the sweater to dry her face before going back in the house.

She sat on the couch for a while and let the visit play over and over in her mind. It felt so good to actually see and hold her daughter and she promised that when she gets her back, they'll never be a part again.

She sat there so long that lots of thoughts went through her head and within thirty minutes, she had decided to go see a lawyer the very next day to start the process of divorcing Manny and she reached out to Shawn. It was time for them to talk.

Chapter Twenty One

"Thank you for calling me. I truly meant what I said when I told you that I want to be there for Camille. My wife and my family as well." Shawn said.

"After everything that has happened, Camille will need a strong support system." Jasmine said.

Shawn told Jasmine that he would call her back when Lori got home so that they can set up a date to meet in person. *"Hopefully one day this week."* He said.

He went to sit on the porch and an hour later, Lori arrived home.

"What has you smiling that big?" She asked.

Shawn wrapped his arms around her and gave her a passionate kiss.

"Shawn we have neighbors." She said.

"I don't care. They can watch me love on my beautiful wife if they want to." He said.

"Let's go in the house so you can tell me what's going on and we maybe can finish what you just started in private." She said.

He smiled and opened the door for her.

"Guess who I just spoke to?" He asked.

Before she could say anything, he blurted out, *"Jasmine! She actually called me. We talked briefly but she said that she wants Camille to know us, all of us."*

"Oh my God Shawn, that's amazing! Our prayers have been answered!" She said.

"I told her that I wanted to speak with her in person but I wanted to see what day is good for you because I want you to be there." He said.

Lori smiled. It felt so good that he wanted to include her. She's just as excited about Camille as everyone else.

Once she got over the pain and anger of learning that Shawn had a child from an affair, Lori prayed for the day that she would be able to have a relationship with the child.

She and Shawn accepted the fact that she couldn't have children but when she found out about Camille, she felt that God was giving her the child she thought she would never have.

Anxious to get the process started, Lori and Shawn agreed that the following day or the day after were good for them to meet with Jasmine.

He gave her a call and confirmed the day after at one o'clock.

           *   *   *

"I'm glad we're getting the intimate side of our relationship back on track." Lori said.

She ran her hand across his bare chest.

He kissed her deeply and caressed her naked body which caused him to get excited again. He started to get on top of her but she stopped him and got on top instead.

They couldn't get enough of each other. Shawn and Lori made love all day and into the night. Only taking a break to use the bathroom or to get something to eat and drink. Sometimes they would do it wherever they were. The bathroom, living room, nor the kitchen was off limits.

"Baby, it's dark outside. We've been at this all day." **Lori laughed.**

"I know and it feels good. I can go all night. I've missed you. We can never let anything disturb our intimacy again." **He said.**

"I agree. Today has been amazing. Not to change the subject but are you going to tell Priscilla about the meeting with Jasmine?" **She said.**

"Yes, I plan to tell her after the meeting. Once you, Jasmine, and I decide how we're going to proceed, I'll set up a time for her to meet the rest of the family. I feel that she needs to meet the family that Camille is a part of. After all that has happened, I want her to feel comfortable with us being in our daughter's life." He said.

"That make sense.." She replied.

*　　　　*　　　　*　　　　*

Shawn, Lori, and Jasmine met for dinner two days later. Shawn was a little nervous bringing both of the ladies together. He knew that his wife was fine with everything but he didn't know what to expect from Jasmine.

He started the conversation with an apology to both of them.

"Hi Jasmine. Thank you for coming. We really appreciate it. Before we get started, I want to say a prayer. Is that okay?" He asked.

Jasmine nodded.

They gathered hands and he began.

"Dear God, I come to you as humbly as I know how. To ask for you to bless this meeting today. You know that we're all hurting right now and we need you to ease our hears and minds today. We need clarity and peace Lord so that we can operate as a family unit for Camille.

Amen"

When everyone took their seats, Shawn continued, *"I have one more thing to say before we begin. First of all, I want to apologize to you again Jasmine. When we met, I knew that I was a married man and I knew that I wanted to stay that way. I had a relationship with you that should have never happened and mostly I want to apologize for how I treated Camille. I'm ashamed of all the things of said to you, including when I said that I never wanted to have anything to do with her, and I'm sorry from the bottom of my heart.*

And Lori I want to apologize to you again too. What I did was wrong but I want you to know that I would never do anything to intentionally hurt you. Thank you for forgiving me and standing by me after finding out what I did. I'm sorry that you had to find out before I was able to tell you. You deserve so much better than that."

Chapter Twenty Two

Jasmine woke up very early that morning. It was just after seven and she was already having a cup of coffee. Although she was nervous about meeting with Shawn and his wife Lori. She was also looking forward to it.

Shawn told her that Lori was fine with everything. She still didn't know what to expect. But Jasmine wondered if Lori would judge her for having an affair with her husband.. Will they blame her for what happened to Camille? She shook her head in an attempt to get rid of the negative thoughts. She tried to stay positive about the meeting by reminding herself that they all just wanted what's best for Camille.

Her cellphone rung and she rushed down the hall to get it from her bedroom. When she looked at the phone, she paused.

The name flashing across the phone was Kelly. Manny's sister finally decided to call.

Jasmine reached out to Kelly the day after James went to jail. She called Kelly five times and left messages but never got a response. As the days passed and more was revealed about him, she realized that Kelly must have known. She reflected on the first time they met, the quietness, and all the strange looks, then realized it was all because of Manny's past.

She was angry that no one told her. Especially since she and Kelly had grown to be so close. She truly loved her like a sister.

Tears started welling up in her eyes so she let the call go to voicemail. *I can't do this right now.* She said and tucked the phone in her back pocket and by the time she made it back to the kitchen, she got the voicemail alert.

Curious to know what she wanted, Jasmine decided to listen to the message.

"Hi Jasmine, I know that you're upset with me for a number of reasons and I'm sorry. You and are great friends...more like sisters and I'm sure you can understand the position that I'm in. James is my brother. No, I don't agree with or condone anything that he has done. He's a sick man and as a matter of fact, I'll probably never speak with him again. I just want you to know that I do still love you and Camille. I just needed time to process it all and get my own emotions in check. I miss you and Camille and I really want to be there from this moment on. Please call me back as soon as you get a chance."

By the time the message was done, tears were streaming down Jasmine's face. She missed Kelly but she had already made up her mind that when she divorces Manny, she's divorcing them too. Since he's really not Camille's father, there's no reason to stay in contact with his family. They knew the kind of monster that he was but by keeping the secret, they put her daughter's welfare in jeopardy.

Whether it was to hurt Kelly or just to clear the air, she wasn't sure of the reason she called her back to tell her about Camille not being her biological niece.

"Hey, I'm glad you called me back." Kelly said.

"Look Kelly, I don't know what prompted you to call me today. You say you love me and Camille but I don't believe that. Not only have you not called for months but you knew he was sick. I remember the look on your face when I told you that I was having a girl. I was so dumb and naive that I ignored all the signs of something being wrong. He told me that there were issues but I never made him tell me what they were because it all happened before me and I figured that it was none of my business! But I want you to know that I've already filed for a divorce from him.

Due to the circumstances, the judge is allowing a quickie divorce so it will be final very soon. With that being said, that means I'm divorcing all of you too." Jasmine said.

Kelly cut her off. *"Jasmine, you can't keep my niece from me! You can't do that! You know how much I love her and she loves me! Don't make me have to fight you in court!"*

"Yes I can and I will. There's something else I need to tell you. I had an affair and Camille isn't even Manny's biological child. I didn't know when we moved her but her father actually lives in this same city. I plan take the necessary steps to have her last name changed, Manny's name removed from the birth certificate, and replace it with her real dad's name. Just forget you've ever known us." Jasmine said then hung up the phone.

Jasmine felt a since of relief. She had so much hurt and anger built up inside and it felt good to finally release some of it.

*   *   *

For the rest of the morning and into the afternoon, Jasmine laid on the couch and watched tv. After her conversation with Kelly, the nervousness of meeting with Shawn and Lori subsided. She looked forward to talking with them and moving forward with the new life she would build for Camille.

Chapter Twenty Three

Shawn rolled over, kissed Lori on her forehead, and pulled her close to him.

"Well good morning to you too." She said then cuddled closer to him.

"Good morning baby. How are you feeling this morning? Are you ready to meet Jasmine?" He asked.

"I'm actually feeling really good about meeting Jasmine I've already forgiven you so forgiving her is easy. My main concern is your daughter. What happened in the past in just that...the past. I'm ready to welcome Camille into our home and love her as if she's my own child."

Shawn knew that Lori struggled with the fact that she was unable to have children and he felt guilty about having a child with another women but he prayed that Camille would fill that void in his wife's life.

After years of pretending she didn't exist, Shawn couldn't stop thinking about Camille. He thought about her every minute of the day. He looked forward to taking her on vacations, to the park, and going to school functions.

"I'm so grateful for you. God truly blessed me when he created you to be my wife and I promise to never hurt you again." He said.

"I believe you. I trust you today just like I did the day I married you. God has already forgiven you and so have I." She replied.

They kissed and shortly after, they were naked. Shawn and Lori made love well into the morning.

          *   *   *   *

After taking a shower, making love again, then taking another shower. Shawn and Lori finally made it to the kitchen to have some breakfast.

"Honey, do you still want eggs and bacon? It's nearly lunch time." Lori asked.

"Yes and coffee." He replied.

She smiled and shook her head as she grabbed the bacon out of the refrigerator and Shawn put a pot of coffee on.

"I guess we need to start working on one of the other bedrooms for Camille huh." She said.

"Yes we do but I'll leave that up to you. I don't know how to decorate for little girls. We can go buy the stuff and I'll help paint and put things together but you'll have to pick everything out." He replied.

"Okay." She laughed. *"How do you think Jasmine is going to feel about Camille living with us?"*

"Well she can't get her right now and I refuse to let her stay in that foster home. I can't imagine her disagreeing." He said.

"Yeah but I'm sure that watching another woman raising her child will be challenging. I'll just have to reassure her that I'm not trying to take her place. She'll always be welcomed to visit Camille and spend time with her whenever she'd like to." She said.

Shawn simply nodded in agreement. He hadn't thought about that but he knew that it would all work out for the good.

They finished breakfast and decided to go shopping for Camille's bedroom to kill some time before their meeting with Jasmine

Chapter Twenty Three

Kevin was worried about his wife. Priscilla would sit for hours in the dark, sharing at the wall. She would be so deep in thought that he would call her name several times before she would answer.

At the current moment, he had to actually touch her to get her attention.

"Honey talk to me. These moments of silence have gotten more frequent and I just want you to know that the kids and I are here for you. I understand that the past few months have been hell but I don't like seeing you like this." He said.

"Kevin, I'm sorry. I don't mean to neglect you or the children. I'm just...I keep replaying this entire situation with Camille, James, and how we've all become intertwined." She said.

"It is like something out of a movie. It's almost unreal but it's real and it's our lives. I will help you deal with this in any way that I

can but have you thought about talking to someone. Like one of your colleagues?" He said.

She was quiet for a moment. Although she agrees that even therapists need to see a therapist at times, she hasn't felt that she needed to speak with anyone.

"Have I been acting that badly?" She asked with tears in her eyes.

"No no come here." He said and held her. *"You've been acting perfectly normal considering what you've been through. I just don't want you to get stuck. We need to find a way to get past this. Especially since Camille is becoming a part of the family. She will be a constant reminder of all of this and we need to be able to deal with it in a positive way."*

The Final Broken Piece   Beverly N. Vercher

"I'm excited about Camille being my niece and I feel that I'm ready to welcome her into our family. I knew the first day I met her that we had a connection.

I felt it in my heart and that's how I knew what was happening to her. I love her already. But you're right. I should talk to someone. I'll make an appointment tomorrow." She said.

"I love you and I want you to be well and happy. Please just talk to me when you're having a bad day. Let me be here for you. Let me hold you when you need to cry. Okay?" He said.

She nodded and laid her head on his chest. Both of them allowed the tears to flow. The stress had become overwhelming and Kevin felt that he needed Priscilla just as badly as she needed him.

He was upset that he couldn't fix this for her. He wanted to take the pain away but he couldn't. He was hurting for her.

*   *   *   *

"She's getting better. Since we talked, she's seen a therapist so she's going in the right direction." Kevin said to Sheryl.

She called him to really see how Priscilla was doing. When she called Priscilla she said she was fine but Sheryl could hear in her voice that something wasn't quite right with her.

"Well good. My baby has been through so much and I've been worried about her. I know she's strong but this situation is enough to break even the strongest person. Please let me know if you guys need anything. Even if you just need me to get the kids so that you can take her out or away for a little weekend getaway to clear your minds. I'm here however you need me." She said.

"I appreciate that and I know Priscilla does too. A little getaway sounds good. I might just take you up on that next weekend. I'll see what Priscilla thinks about it and let you know." He replied.

A few moments after hanging up with Sheryl he received a call from Pastor Rachel. He wasn't surprised.

"I just called to pray with you Kevin." She said.

"Sure. We're always in need for some additional prayers." He replied.

Father God we come to you with our heads bowed and hearts humbled. We come in faith asking for your grace Father. We come on behalf of our beloved Priscilla. God please heal the pain in her heart and in her mind. Please keep her covered in times that she feels confused and keep her focused in times that she feels lost. We know that you can do all things so we are thanking you in advance for your grace and mercy. We thank you for the healing that's about to take place.

We count it done in the name of Jesus.

Amen

Chapter Twenty Four

Shawn and Lori arrived at the restaurant fifteen minutes early. They were seated about five minutes before Jasmine arrived.

"Hi I'm Jasmine." She said greeting Lori.

"Hi I'm Lori. Nice to meet you." Lori replied and they shook hands.

"Hello Jasmine." Shawn said.

"Hi Shawn. I want to thank both of you for agreeing to speak with me about Camille." Jasmine said.

"Jasmine, Shawn and I want you to know that we are excited about being in Camille's life. I forgave him for what happened a long time ago and we're ready to do what's right for her. In no way whatsoever will I ever try to take your place as her mother but I will be the best bonus mom that I can be. We are family now and not only are we here for her but you too." Lori said.

"Thank you so much." Jasmine replied.

"I want to first apologize to you again for not wanting to be in Camille's life. I was trying to protect myself and my marriage. Not taking in consideration that she may need my protection as well. I have so many regrets but I promise you that I will spend the rest of my life protecting her. I haven't been able to think of anything else for the past few months. I'm ready to have her in my life...our lives." Shawn said then looked at Lori and smiled.

For the next two hours, as they enjoyed dinner, Jasmine explained the entire process of getting Camille out of foster care. They will have to meet with the counselor, the victim's advocate then they'll get a date for a court hearing with the judge who makes the final decision.

"So what are we looking at? Another ninety days or so?" Shawn asked.

"Probably so. Another day is too long for me but we are at the mercy of the system right now. But the good thing is that we'll get visitations and phone calls." Jasmine said.

"How have you been holding up? I know that this is hard for you. Are you okay?" Lori asked.

Jasmine could tell that she' genuinely concerned. *"Thanks for your concern. When it all first happened, I was a mess. I mean a mess but I knew that I had to get myself together so that I could work on getting her back home."*

"And what about Jam...Manny?" Shawn asked.

"Our divorce will be final in a few weeks but from what I understand, he's dying. He has Stage 4 Stomach Cancer and only has a short time left." Jasmine said.

"How do you feel about that?" Lori asked.

"I feel like he can't die soon enough for me. He destroyed my daughter's life. He destroyed my life." Jasmine replied.

"You have every right to be angry. What he did was horrendous but he's still one of God's children and we must pray for him. God is the only one with the power to decide his fate. He will be held accountable for his actions but we have to keep our hearts and our conscious clear so that we can be forgiven when we step outside of God's expectations of us. We must not wish a horrible death on him. We must pray that he repents and finds his way to Jesus before he leaves this earth. God will decide whether he deserves to go to Heaven or Hell. We don't have that kind of power over someone ease's life but or actions can cause our own fate to be shifted." Lori said.

They sat quietly for a moment.

Then Shawn said, *"I understand how you feel Jasmine. I had to ask God to forgive me for all the thoughts I was having about him. But our faith won't allow us to wish ill will on anyone. We will pray that when he takes his last breath, there is no pain and he has peace."* Shawn said.

"I guess after all I've been through, my faith isn't where it should be. I don't understand how God could let this happen to us. I just don't." Jasmine said.

"Since we are a family now, I want to invite you to attend church with us. We can even do some counseling sessions with our pastor just to keep our family unite covered and blessed." Lori said.

"Yes, I'd love to. I'm willing to do anything that will help get my life back in order and to be happy. Truly happy again with my daughter back home." Jasmine said.

Chapter Twenty Five

Jasmine went straight home, took a long hot bath, then drank some herbal tea while she watched tv. She felt good after the meeting with Shawn and Lori and she knew that they would be good for Camille. She smiled as she thought about their future.

She definitely planned to start going to church with them. Eventually she'll find her own church but for now, she thinks it would be good to go with them, as well as the counseling.

She went to the kitchen to place her cup in the sink and on her way back to her room, she stopped and looked in Camille's room. She imagined her little girl happily playing in her room again. Then being able to sleep peacefully at night without worrying about anyone hurting her.

Jasmine looked forward to the day that she'll wake up early and make them breakfast. She missed her daughter terribly.

She went back to her room and realized that she had a missed call. Her phone was still on silent since dinner. The call was from Kelly. *Why in the world would she call me? I have nothing else to say to her.* She said out loud and shook her head.

"Jasmine, this is Kelly. I know that you probably didn't answer on purpose and that's okay. I'm just calling to let you know that they are placing James in a Hospice Care Facility. He's declining quicker than they expected and the doctor's are now saying that he might only make it another week. If that. I had not intentions of ever speaking to him again but I can't let him die alone. They say that he's asking for you so if you would like to visit him with me, I would love that. Listen, I don't care what you said. Camille is and always will be my niece. I love that little girl like she's my own child. Please call me back so that we can talk. Love you bye."

Jasmine deleted the message then blocked Kelly's number.

Why does she think that I would want to go visit that man that molested my daughter? What they hell is she thinking? That entire family is crazy.

As she laid in bed, she started thinking about Manny and decided to do some research on him since she never really knew who he was.

She put his real name in the Google search bar and after three hours of reading different news articles, she was stunned. She had discovered that not only is his victim Camille's therapist but her aunt as well. Just to make sure she wasn't mistaken, she found Shawn on Facebook and looked through his photos and it was confirmed that Dr. Walton is in fact his sister.

*   *   *   *

With so many questions going through her head, she barely got any sleep the night before. She wanted to ask Shawn about it but she didn't know how he would respond so she decided to make and appointment to speak with her directly. She called the office and was able to get in that same day at four. She told her assistant that he wanted to follow up with her about Camille since she would be coming home soon.

"Follow me Mrs. Rollins." Amanda said.

Jasmine hated being called Mrs. Rollins. She couldn't wait until the divorce was final to change back to her maiden name, Coyle.

"Hi Dr. Walton. Thanks for seeing me at such a short notice." Jasmine said as she sat in the seat in front of her desk.

"You're very welcome." Priscilla said.

"I came in to talk to you about Camille." Jasmine said. Carefully watching Priscilla's expression.

"Yes, how is she?" Priscilla asked.

"She's okay. Ready to come home. Dr. Walton, I hope I'm not crossing the line but I really wanted to talk to you because I recently learned that not only did my soon to be ex husband molest you when you were younger but you're Camille's aunt. You're her biological father's sister. How long have you known?"

Jasmine asked.

Priscilla sat quietly for a few seconds before speaking. She was trying her best to keep her emotions intact. *"I've known for quite some time now. Shawn brought the whole family together and told us about her. As you can imagine, I was shocked. God truly works in mysterious ways. Out of all the therapists in our city, she ends up in my office. When Shawn told us about her, it didn't surprise me. I've stated several times that I felt an instant connection with her. Something inside me knew she was special. I'm looking forward to having her in our lives."* Priscilla said.

The Final Broken Piece   Beverly N. Vercher

"I'm so grateful to all of you for accepting her so openly. I know that the entire situation is somewhat ugly but I see that something beautiful will come out of it. I'm so sorry for what happened to you but I'm glad that Camille will have you, a survivor of molestation by the same man. You will be vital in helping her move on with her life and become successful in any thing she wants to do." Jasmine said.

"We are family now so I want to be completely honest with you. This has been hard for me. Not finding out about my niece but the entire situation with James. He took so much from us. Because of what he did to me, my mother was charged with neglect and when she was told that she may never get us back, she committed suicide. When I found out that he was the person hurting Camille, it brought back all the memories and the emotions were as if it had happened to me all over again. Then I find out that she's actually my niece. My goodness, it broke my heart. I want you to

know that we don't blame you in any way and I'm glad that the court system didn't either. I was also so afraid for you because of what we went through with our mother." Priscilla said.

Jasmine fought back the tears welling up in her eyes. She could see the pain on Priscilla's face and her heart broke for her. *"I'm so sorry Dr. Walton. Thank you for thinking of me through all of your own pain. That man is a monster and I don't feel sorry at all that he's dying. I'm sorry for saying that to you. I know that your family is very spiritual. I learned that from speaking with Shawn and Lori but I'm not on that level yet. I'm glad that he'll never be able to hurt anyone else again."* Jasmine continued to tell her about the diagnosis and the fact that James had a short time to live. Priscilla didn't respond but she said a silent prayer asking that God forgive her for the feeling of joy she had inside.

Jasmine continued, *"I'm just glad that out of all of this tragedy comes triumph for Camille and Shawn. It brought them together and I couldn't be happier. Well, Dr. Walton, I'm going to leave. I know you're a busy woman. Thank you for taking the time to see me today and I'm looking forward to seeing you again soon. Hopefully I'll have my baby girl with me."*

"It was my pleasure and I'm looking forward to seeing both of you again soon." **Priscilla replied.**

Chapter Twenty Six

"Mr. Rollins, Mr. Rollins, can you hear me?" The doctor shouted.

James was transported to the hospital after being unresponsive when the guards tried to wake him for roll call that morning.

He could hear the doctor calling his name but it sounded very far away and when he tries to speak, nothing comes out. His vision was very blurry so he was unable to tell where he was who was speaking to him.

"Mr. Rollins, my name is Dr. Jacobs. Blink your eyes if you can hear me." He said.

James blinked.

Dr. Jacobs shined a light in his eyes. *"Blink again for me if you saw that."*

James blinked.

The room was busy with nurses, checking his blood pressure, poking him with needles, checking him temperature, and everything else the doctor asked them to do.

James couldn't feel much of what they were doing to him. He tried to focus on the faces but he still couldn't and before he knew it, he was out.

"The medication will probably have him asleep for the rest of the night so we'll just monitor his blood pressure and temperature every two to three hours." Dr. Jacobs said.

"Does he have any family we can call? I don't see anyone listed on his paperwork." One of the nurses asked the other.

"No, I asked the guard that escorted him here and he said all of the information is on his paperwork from the jail but no one is listed on those either." The other nurse replied.

They both shook their heads.

"So many people go to jail or prison and their families just forget about them and they die alone." The first nurse stated.

They continued to make note on his chart and go over the information that was provided by the guard.

"It wouldn't have anything in the documentation that tells us what he's in jail for." The first nurse stated as she noticed the second nurse peering over the paperwork.

"Regardless of what he's done, I just think that it's sad that he's probably going to die soon and no one is here to say goodbye." The first nurse continued.

The second nurse didn't respond but she totally disagreed. She felt that if he was a murderer, he deserved to die alone.

They finished their tasks. Then turned out the light and left the room.

Chapter Twenty Seven

Jasmine received a call from someone at the jail advising her that her husband was being placed in a hospice facility. The female explained that the cancer has spread to his liver and kidneys and that it's just a matter of time until he passes away.

"I'm not sure if you're aware of this but our divorce will be final in two days and I should no longer be on his list of contacts." She said.

"I'm sorry. I didn't know. I have you still listed as his wife. I will make sure we get this updated and I'll try to call he other names on the list. Have a good day Mrs. Rollins." The nurse said before hanging up.

Jasmine sat still for a moment. She wasn't sure how to feel. Memories of when they met replayed in her mind. She still couldn't believe that the man she loved so intensely would destroy her life. Tears rolled down her face.

Over the past few weeks, she had taken Lori's offer to attend church with them. They had even had one counseling session with their pastor who is also Shawn's grandmother.

Jasmine thinks that being around them has softened her up a little when it comes to Manny and that's why she was crying.

Dear God, I know that you haven't heard from me in a while and for that, I'm asking for your forgiveness. I come to you today, not for myself but for Manny...James. I ask that you forgive him. I ask that you accept him into your arms and show him the way to glory. What he's done was once unforgivable to me but I know that you are a forgiving God and that's what he needs and he takes his final breath. Please give him peace and understanding as transitions from this earth. Right now I just want to say thank you and I'm counting it done. In Jesus name. Amen

The Final Broken Piece   Beverly N. Vercher

She paced the floor as thoughts of the past few months swirled through her head. Her life had changed drastically. One day she's married with a beautiful daughter and the next her daughter is ripped from her arms and her husband goes to jail for molesting her.

The fact that Manny was dying alone didn't bother her. He hurt so many people, including his own family; who does he expect to be there? Just because he's dying doesn't mean he'll be forgiven to the point where we'll be surrounded by people crying and wishing he was leaving them.

The sadness and depression of what he did almost made Jasmine want to give up but she knew that she had to keep fighting for Camille.

Tears continued to fall but she was able to smile when she thought about her daughter finally getting the chance to have her biological father in her life. They are a good Christian family; what Camille will need to heal.

The ringing of her phone snapped her out of her train of thought.

She paused when she saw that it was her sister calling. She hadn't spoken to her family for a very long time.

Their relationship was strained ever since she married Manny and moved away. She figured Lisa was calling because they've found out what happened. Unsure if she would be judgmental, Jasmine wasn't sure if she was ready to talk to her. *I'll probably never be ready,* she thought out loud then answered.

"Hello." Jasmine said.

"Hey Jas. It's me, Lisa. How are you?" Lisa said.

"Hi Lisa, I'm okay. How have you been?" Jasmine replied.

"Pretty good. Jas, I know that it has been a long time since we've spoken and I want to apologize." Lisa said.

The Final Broken Piece   Beverly N. Vercher

"No Lisa, all of you where just trying to protect me. I'm sorry for turning my back and not keeping in touch." Jasmine said.

"We love you and just wanted the best for you but I feel that it could have been handled differently on both ends. Anyway, I called you to let you know about mom. She's showing the early signs of Dementia and lately she has been asking about you and Camille. So, I am hoping that you and my niece can come visit soon. How is she? I know that she has gotten so big." Lisa said.

Jasmine paused for a moment. She realized that her family still doesn't know about everything that has occurred. *Then again, how could they?* Jasmine thought to herself.

"Well a lot has happened in the past nine months. A lot..." Jasmine said ad over the next hour, she explained everything to

her younger sister. By the time she was done, they both were crying.

"*I still want to come and see mom. I have to make peace with her. I don't want her to know about all of this. It will upset her too much. But, I need to speak with my attorney and the social workers to see where things are with the case. Then I'll be able to decide the best time to leave town for a couple of days. I'll have to let Camille's father know that I'm leaving too. I'll call you back in a day or so with an update.*" Jasmine replied.

"*Okay, I totally understand. I look forward to hearing from you in a few days. Love you.*" Lisa said.

"*Love you too.*" Jasmine said.

Chapter Twenty Eight

Jasmine smiled when she looked around the room. It was full of love and support for her and Camille.

Shawn, Lori, Priscilla, Kevin, Sheryl, Tiana, Brandy, Pastor Rachel, and Lisa. Who had flown in after their aunt agreed to take care of their mother for a few days.

It was a very important day. The day that they would go to court in an attempt to get Camille out of foster care.

Although Jasmine was confident that her daughter was coming home, she was still very nervous.

She prayed more that day than she has in the last month and Pastor Rachel prayed long and hard when they all arrived to the courthouse.

Tears flowed around the room but mostly they were joyful tears.

Everyone was excited that Camille was coming home and they

were all ready to start this new chapter in their lives.

"Ready?" The attorney said when she peeked in the door.

Jasmine nodded and Pastor Rachel said, *"It's in God's hands now and we must trust that he will do what's best for her."*

The hearing was expected to last most of the day. Jasmine had a good relationship with the social workers but their job was to protect Camille and because they couldn't discuss the case, she wasn't sure if they felt that she should have her back.

The judge came in, made his announcement and the hearing began.

She sat between Priscilla and Pastor Rachel. They comforted her by holding her hands. They listened to the details of why Camille was in foster care and it took all of Jasmine's strength to hold back the tears. She kept reminding herself that it's just part of the process. Camille is no longer in danger. Not because the monster who did that to her died but because she vowed to never let that happen to her baby again. Even if it means not getting into another relationship until Camille is grown.

*   *   *

A week after receiving the call that Manny was going into hospice, he passed away. He was alone. His body was never claimed so he was buried in the prison cemetery

He had written Jasmine one last letter. She had thrown the previous letters away without opening them but she decided to read the last one because she knew it was his last dying wish.

Dear Jasmine,

I know that I am the last person that you want to hear from right now. So, if you're reading this, I want to say thank you. This letter isn't to ask for your forgiveness. What I did was unforgivable and

The Final Broken Piece — Beverly N. Vercher

I know that everything I'm going through is my punishment and I deserve it all.

I'm writing this letter for Camille. I want to tell her how sorry I am for what I did to her and to let her know that it wasn't her fault. Nothing she did or said had anything to do with what happened. I'm a sick man that's why I've accepted death. I deserve to die for what I've done to her and other little girls like her. I know that it will take time but she'll be okay and with me gone, it will make her healing even easier.

I was shocked when I found out that she wasn't my biological child but that didn't stop me from loving her. And looking back, I'm glad she's not mine. Now you can truly be rid of me. I'm not someone who should be remembered because memories of me only bring pain to everyone who's ever known me. So I want to be forgotten. This is not a cry for sympathy. This is just acknowledging what I've done and apologizing for my actions.

The Final Broken Piece   Beverly N. Vercher

Jasmine, you are an amazing woman and mother. Camille is very lucky to have you.

I know that she will be back with you soon and I pray that you're able to find the happiness that they both of you deserve.

Goodbye my love.

Jasmine tucked the letter in a keepsake box and placed in the back of her closet. When Camille got older. She would show it to her.

    *   *   *

Mary cried as she reached for her daughter. She was in the early stages of Dementia but at that moment, she recognized Jasmine as if she had just seen her the day before.

"It's good to see you Mama. How have you been?" Jasmine asked.

"I'm good. How you?" Mary replied.

"I'm fine. I'm sorry that it has been so long since I've visited. I love you so much Mama." Jasmine said then hugged her mother.

Her mother didn't realized how long it had been. She actually thought that she had just seen her a few weeks prior. Jasmine didn't correct her. She just smiled.

That visit was three days and after she returned home, Jasmine called her every day and promised to visit again soon and bring Camille with her.

*   *   *

"I don't see any reason that the child should not be returned to her mother. Mrs. Rollins has completed everything that was asked of her. Upon investigating, we found that she had absolutely no contact with Mr. Rollins, who is now deceased, after his arrest. When home visit were conducted, the home was always neat and tidy. Camille has her own room and plenty of space to live

comfortably and grown. She has also been reunited with her biological paternal family who are all upstanding members of the community. We don't see any concerns whatsoever for her care and well being while in the custody of her mother.

We are prepared to allow Camille to return home today if you agree Your Honor." Darla Mathis, the caseworker with Child Protective Services, explained.

The judge agreed and Camille was scheduled to return home that day. Everyone was so excited. Once they got outside of the courtroom, they cried, hugged and thanked God.

Then about thirty minutes later, Camille came walking down the hall holding the hand of a social worker that she hadn't seen before.

"Mommy mommy!" Camille yelled as she ran towards her mother.

Jasmine held her tight and kissed her over and over again. *"Yes baby, you're coming home."*

The case manager allowed Shawn and Lori to attend the last three visits that Camille and Jasmine had. She didn't want everyone to be complete strangers when she did get to go home.

"Hi." Camille said shyly as she hugged her father and stepmother.

"Hey there beautiful." Shawn replied.

"Camille, this is my sister, your aunt Lisa and do you remember Dr. Walton? Well come to find out, she's actually your aunt too. She's your father's sister. This is your uncle Kevin, aunt Tiana, grandmother Sheryl, your great aunt, Brandy and great grandmother Rachel." Jasmine said.

They all hugged her.

"You can call me Nana." Pastor Rachel said.

"And I'm your Mimi.*"* Sheryl stated.

THE END

The Final Broken Piece   Beverly N. Vercher

Writing this book gave me so much joy. I had no idea that I would be returning to the lives of Sheryl, Shawn, and Priscilla. I thought Shattered but not Broken was the end. But just like in real life, things can happen that brings the past to the present and we can only pray that we have the strength to handle it.

Sadly child molestation and domestic sexual abuse happens everyday. There are children, teens, and young adults living in fear everyday. Although this story was about a little girl, boys are victims too.

As parents we wear many hats. We have to work and handle our responsibilities on a daily basis. We carry the roles as wives, mothers, sisters, aunties, and so many others. So, of course we can't see everything. That's why we must stress the importance of communication to our children at very young ages. You want them to be able to talk to you about absolutely anything.

The Final Broken Piece   Beverly N. Vercher

No matter who threatens them! I remember having a conversation about this with my older sister, Sandra, when I was younger. She said, *"Even if they threaten to kill me, tell me, because I would rather die fighting for you, than to live with someone hurting you."* That stuck to me and when I grew up and had my own children, I totally understood how she felt.

Some subjects are hard to talk about but you must have an open dialog with your children.

There are books and videos available to at least open the door so that the discussion can begin. They need to feel comfortable in knowing that they can come to you. Even when threatened with bodily harm.

Listen to them & believe them no matter who it is! You would be surprised at who the demons are lurking in some families.

Also, pay attention to their actions. Have they changed?

Maybe they were once very friendly and outgoing but now they're reserved and shy. Especially around certain people. If they once were excited to go with someone but now they cry...ASK QUESTIONS!

Your children depend on you to do more than just feed and clothe them....

I pray that you enjoyed reading this book just as much as I enjoyed writing it.

Love Always,

Beverly N. Vercher

contact@beverlynvercheronline.com

www.beverlynvercheronline.com

FOLLOW ME:

Facebook: Author Beverly N. Vercher

Instagram: @VerchUUsGifts

Twitter: @BNVercher

Also follow my business pages:

Clash Beauty Brand

www.clashbeautybrand.com

Facebook: Clash Beauty Brand

Instagram: @ClashBeautyBrand

Twitter: @BeautyClash

The Final Broken Piece   Beverly N. Vercher

www.ingramcontent.com/pod-product-compliance
Lightning Source LLC
Chambersburg PA
CBHW032032040426
42449CB00007B/865